POACHER'S MOON

POACHER'S MOON

By

William Wasserman

Copyright © July 2023 by Penn's Woods Publications

A Penn's Woods Book

ISBN: 979-8-218-18835-1

The stories herein were inspired by actual events; however, I admit to taking substantial creative liberties and to re-creating dialog, places, businesses, and events. I have given the characters fictitious names and have altered their physical descriptions, and any resemblance to actual persons, living or dead, businesses, companies, or events is entirely coincidental.

For Edward F. Bond

My friend, mentor, and game warden extraordinaire.

Ah, pray make no mistake,
We are not shy;
We are very wide awake,
The moon and I!
>   — Sir William Schwenck Gilbert
>   *The Mikado* [1885], act 1

x

There goes my hero
Watch him as he goes...
          ~Song by Foo Fighters

A LONG PASSAGE INTO NIGHT

IT WAS THE FIRST DAY of small game season for squirrels and grouse as State Game Warden Chuck Arcovitch steered his four-wheel-drive patrol vehicle slowly along the rutted and broken dirt road. In the distance, a rising sun began to peek over the Endless Mountains casting an amber glow through the open woods that walled the narrow roadway on both sides.

Hunting pressure was always light during small game season in northeastern Pennsylvania, and Susquehanna County was no exception. This was big game country, rural and mountainous, with most people living in several of the long and narrow valleys where good farmland was abundant.

The county was named after the Susquehanna River, geologically considered to be the oldest major river system in the world (older than the Nile, which is thirty million years old). It is made up of over eight hundred square miles with ninety-nine percent being rural.

Chuck was one of two state game wardens assigned to the county. And although his district covered more than four hundred square miles, he didn't expect much activity as he cruised the rolling hills in the western end of his district. In fact, he would have been surprised to come across any hunters at all.

There was little interest in killing squirrels for most hunters here, and while the ruffed grouse had been Pennsylvania's

11

official state bird since 1931, the population had been on the decline for years and they were rarely seen. Consequently, true dyed-in-the-wool grouse hunters were almost nonexistent in his district.

Although archery deer season had opened a month before, Chuck did not expect to check many bow hunters this morning either. They were few and far between, and those who were afield would be on stand somewhere in the woods by now. Walking in on a bow hunter and ruining a potential shot at a nice whitetail is never a good idea unless you're investigating a tip on a violation like hunting over bait. Today, Chuck had no inside information on unlawful hunting activity anywhere in his district.

Rifle deer season would open in several weeks, and that's when things would really pick up. Until then, Chuck expected most days to be relatively quiet unless there was a hunting accident somewhere. Investigating hunting related shooting incidents could be extremely time consuming. And though it was interesting to piece everything together and come up with the specifics behind how the shooting took place, there was a huge downside as the more serious cases often resulted in tragedy and heartbreak. Most game wardens hoped they would get through the entire hunting season without any hunting accidents in their district.

Chuck came to a crossroad at the end of the potholed dirt lane and considered whether to turn left or right, east or west. Catching poachers while on routine patrol, he knew, was mostly about luck and circumstance. A simple and spontaneous decision on which direction to go might make the difference between apprehending an outlaw hunter or spending the day spinning his wheels and burning gasoline with nothing to show for his efforts.

He sat at the intersection staring through the windshield at the rolling fields before him that had once been thriving farmland. The pastures that had produced hundreds of acres of corn and wheat had long since reverted to a waving sea of switchgrass and invasive weeds. A vacant and dilapidated barn, the sagging roof covered with a heavy morning frost, was all that verified its once thriving past. The accompanying farmhouse that stood by the roadway for generations had been burned to the ground by vandals long ago.

The landscape here was bleak.

Chuck took a pair of Ray-Ban Aviator sunglasses from his shirt pocket and slipped them on.

He turned east into the sun.

He had only traveled a few miles when a call came over his mobile radio: *"Dallas to five-three-five..."*

Chuck reached for the microphone connected to a hook on the dashboard and put it to his face. "Five-three-five by."

"The state police want you to meet them for a suspected deer violation," a dispatcher replied. *"They're at a house on Route 167. It's three miles south of the village of Brooklyn. You'll see their car parked in the driveway."*

Chuck recognized the voice. "Ten-four, Barney," he said. "Tell them I'll be there in twenty minutes."

It's not uncommon to receive calls from state and local police departments concerning game violations they've discovered while investigating other offenses. Most poachers are reprobates that don't just violate wildlife laws, and Chuck had no idea what he was in for. Dispatchers are trained not to give too much information over the radio about violations. Too many outlaws are scanning the airwaves, and word travels fast. Barney kept it short: "a suspected deer violation," he had said. Nothing more. As a result, Chuck couldn't help but ponder the possibilities: One deer? Two or more? How many poachers were involved? Did the state troopers have them corralled or would he spend days putting together a complicated case? A thousand thoughts raced through his mind as he made his way toward the suspect's house.

Minutes after passing through the small village of Brooklyn at the northern end of his district, he spotted a white Ford Crown Victoria parked in a driveway on his left. It was marked STATE POLICE in bold lettering across the trunk and had the Pennsylvania state seal displayed on the door facing him. Its emergency lightbar flashed a rapid-fire strobe of red and blue that reflected off the rundown two-story house directly in front of it. A state trooper stood in the driveway as Chuck pulled onto the property.

The yard was overgrown with weeds and looked like it hadn't been mowed in months. A naked maple tree stood alongside the house, its leaves covering the ground in a thick blanket of red and orange under a clear blue sky. Chuck parked behind the trooper's car and climbed out of his vehicle to greet him. There was a crisp chill in the air as he stepped across curled leaves that crunched under his boots. They shook hands. The trooper's name was Aaron Rusk. Chuck had worked with him a number of times in the past, most recently in a hunting accident probe that had started as a murder investigation.

"Chuck, you're not going to believe this place," said Rusk. "Hope you haven't had breakfast yet."

"That bad?"

"Worse."

"What's going on inside?" asked Chuck.

"Guy's name is Donald Brown. He's a dopehead with priors. We have a search warrant for the property and found venison in the refrigerator. Thought you might want to check it out. He admits he doesn't have a hunting license."

"I'll go have a talk with him," said Chuck.

"The place is disgusting," cautioned the trooper. "Just be prepared."

The trooper had given Chuck enough reason to get a search warrant of his own, but instead of wasting time driving back to town to meet with the district attorney and then the local judge, he grabbed a CONSENT TO SEARCH FORM from a briefcase in his patrol car before meeting with the suspect.

As he walked into the house, he was hit with the sickly-sweet smell of human filth and decay. Shades were drawn on all the windows except one from which a single shaft of sunlight spilled into the darkened room and lighted dust particles that floated in the air. An elderly man sat on a worn and tattered couch with coiled springs poking through the fabric. "Come on in," the man offered. His voice warm and friendly.

"I'm with the Pennsylvania Game Commission," Chuck said as he stepped across a threadbare area rug that hadn't been vacuumed in years. "Your name sir?"

"Donald Brown," he replied. "But you can call me Don. I prefer the shorter version."

He was in his mid-sixties with a pudgy alcoholic face and clearly in need of a bath. His gray hair was plastered to his head from lack of a good washing, and he had a thin white beard that was stained yellow down both sides. He was dressed in a bulky plaid work shirt and ragged jeans soiled with greasy black stains.

Chuck said, "Don, I'm here because the state police found venison in your refrigerator. Do you have a hunting license?"

"Didn't think I needed one for a roadkilled deer," he said.

It was the typical answer most outlaws used when you found them in unlawful possession of deer meat.

"So, you're saying the venison is from a roadkill," Chuck said evenly.

"That's right. Picked it up with my son last week. Him and his friends stay here every once in a while."

Chuck explained to Don that he should have contacted the Game Commission for a permit if the deer was a roadkill, and that it was a violation to be in possession of the meat without one. He told him that he intended to search the house, garage, and outlying property, for which Don agreed to sign the CONSENT TO SEARCH FORM that Chuck had brought with him. Don was laid back and impassive about the whole thing, and Chuck suspected that he had burned himself out on drugs and alcohol long ago.

Chuck started his search with the kitchen. There was a utility room next to it, approximately six-by-six feet, with empty beer cans piled three feet high across the floor. Chuck

15

noticed he couldn't detect much of a stale beer smell because an assortment of other odors, which he couldn't identify at the time, drowned out the sour smell of the beer. The kitchen was disgusting. Splatters of dried food stained the walls, and the cheap linoleum floor was covered with a thin film of brown grime. There was a Formica countertop to his left stacked with magazines and old newspapers that had yellowed from age. The sink was filled to the top with dishes encrusted with food, as there was no running water or electricity in the house.

When Chuck went to the refrigerator and opened it, a waft of warm putrid air hit him in the face like a brick. He winced and stepped back, covering his nose and mouth with his hand. The fridge was empty save the skinned hindquarter of a deer, its rotting flesh writhing with bright yellow maggots. Chuck quickly closed the door, but the awful stench lingered in his nose and in his mouth as he walked back into the living room.

Don sat on his couch as Chuck approached him for the second time. There was an overwhelming musty odor in the room, like the one he had smelled many times when entering homes that had been flooded by Hurricane Agnes years ago.

"I'm going upstairs to look around," he said. "Do you want to accompany me."

Don shook his head. "No, I'll stay right here," he said wearily. "Nothing up there is mine, anyway. My son and his friends use those rooms. I sleep right here on the couch."

As Chuck climbed the stairs toward the second floor, shiny reddish-brown cockroaches scurried for cover. The stairway walls were smashed and crumbling, and he envisioned people high on drugs and alcohol falling against the walls or smashing them with their fists or other objects out of some form of psychotic rage.

There were two bedrooms upstairs, both void of furniture with the exception of a single bare mattress in each room. The hardwood floors were covered with a gritty kind of soil and littered with dirty clothes that had been tossed into loose piles here and there. Empty potato chip bags, candy wrappers, crushed cigarette packs, and other assorted junk was strewn about the floors.

Walking into the bathroom across the hall, he almost gagged. A cluster of bloated flies circled a toilet piled high with human feces. It was all he could do to keep from vomiting. Chuck had been to some bad places before, but nothing that compared with this. He had to get out of the house and get some air. No water, no electricity, and no money to be spent except for drugs and alcohol; therefore, no concern for cleanliness, he thought. Not that that was an excuse for the abject squalor the occupants chose to live in.

He went back down the stairs and stepped out the front door without so much as a glance back at Don sitting in the dark on his moth-eaten couch. Once outside, he filled his lungs with fresh air, glad to be out of the place.

Chuck walked around the side of the house toward the detached garage to look for additional deer parts when he observed more human feces piled up below the two upstairs bedroom windows he'd visited before. Apparently, once the toilet had filled, the windows were used as some kind of grotesque open-air outhouse. *How in the world could people live like this?* he asked himself.

Moving on to the garage, Chuck noticed that it too had been neglected just like the rest of the property. Strips of moldy white paint peeled off the wooden structure in long ribbons. The overhead door lay detached and broken on the concrete floor, its four windows reduced to jagged shards of glass that winked back at him as he inspected the interior. The building hadn't been used for a very long time and was wide open. Chuck could see all he needed right from the open doorway, there was no illegal game or animal parts to be found anywhere inside.

On the way back to the house, he spoke briefly to Trooper Rusk and then climbed into his patrol car and drove back onto the state highway, heading east once again to resume his patrol. He couldn't find it in his heart to prosecute Don for picking up a roadkill and not obtaining a permit for it. Even if he did, Chuck knew he wouldn't pay the fine, since the little money he had was spent on drugs, beer, and food—probably in that order. It was just another one of those cases involving destitute human beings that law enforcement officers often see, and he knew there was no way to help people like that unless they were willing to make the first move. He would file a report with the proper health authorities later in the week, he thought, hoping they would provide additional food resources for Don along with a wellness evaluation.

As he cruised down the macadam state road, background chatter began to accelerate across his mobile radio concerning game law violations from neighboring districts. Perhaps things would pick up after all, he thought. And it was at that very moment that a dispatcher reached out to him.

"Deputy Bill Swanson wants you to meet him regarding a poaching incident," the dispatcher said. *"Get to a phone as soon as you can, and I'll relay the information."*

Deputy Bill Swanson had been out all night and was finishing an investigation of his own while Chuck had been searching Donald Brown's house and property for illegal game. At five-foot-eleven and one hundred ninety-five pounds, Swanson was a big man and strong as an ox, even while still in his fifties. He was well known in the eastern section of Chuck's district, and would often get calls about poaching activity.

And so it was, when shortly after midnight, a man named Richard Harlin heard a single shot from a high-powered rifle and suspected that someone was targeting deer. The shot was close by, and Harlin knew the field up the road from his house was loaded with deer almost every night. He rolled out of bed, jumped into a pair of jeans, and ran out the front door while still buttoning his shirt. He saw a van stopped along the road by the field fifty yards away with its lights turned off. He didn't know anyone living in the area who had a van, and suspected they were up to no good.

Despite the fact that he hadn't put on shoes in his rush out the door, Harlin sprinted barefooted toward the vehicle hoping to get a good look at it, the bottoms of his feet stinging on the ice-cold macadam road. Halfway there, the van's headlights lit up and he heard the clunk of a transmission being engaged. He suspected the vehicle was about to take off and ran as fast as he could, almost reaching it as it sped away. A two-tone Ford van with New York tags. Harlin made a mental note of the license number and hurried back to his house to call the police.

After reporting what he had found to the state police, they ran the plate and contacted Deputy Swanson. In Pennsylvania, troopers are authorized to enforce all laws of the commonwealth, including game and wildlife laws, but they usually turn those investigations over to the local district game warden or a deputy when they receive information about poaching and other unlawful hunting activities, which is what they did in this case.

After receiving a call from the state police, Swanson telephoned Richard Harlin to set up a meeting, then drove out to his house and spoke with him. Even though it was after midnight, Harlin was glad that the deputy came by.

"I think whoever was in that van shot at a deer," Harlin told him. "They were probably about to go look for it when they saw me coming from behind them."

"Where was the van when you saw it?" asked Swanson.

"Just give me a minute to get shoes and a coat on," he said. "It was just up the road a bit; I'll take you there."

Deputy Swanson thumbed on his five-cell Maglite and bathed the field with its beam. There was no wind, making it easier to hear as he walked the field's perimeter searching for a dead deer or a trace of blood in the grass. In the distance, he heard the deep, soft, rhythmic hoots of a great horned owl. *Hoo-h'Hoo-hoo-hoo.* His passion for the outdoors was why he became a deputy years ago. It was why he was out here tonight searching for anything that might lead him to the poachers who were operating in the area. Under the bright full moon, they wouldn't have needed a spotlight to locate any deer grazing in the field close to the road. It was a time when night hunting was always most active.

Deputy Swanson circled the perimeter of the field, scanning the adjacent woodland with his light as he searched. He made a dozen loops, methodically working his way to the center, but there was no sign of a deer being taken. No blood, no carcass, nothing. He walked back to the road and searched the macadam for a spent cartridge but came up empty once again. If they shot at a deer as Richard Harlan had said, they probably missed. Hoping he might discover the poachers still in the area, Swanson returned to his vehicle and began to cruise the neighboring backroads. He planned to stay out all night if necessary. Because there was no sign that a deer had been killed, he was sure the poachers were still on the hunt somewhere close by.

It was Jake McGurk who had spotted Richard Harlan sprinting toward them in his bare feet earlier. He was sitting in the passenger's seat of the van after taking a shot at a deer when he caught sight of him in the sideview mirror. "Let's get out of here, Ricky!" he cried. "Somebody's coming!"

Ricky Lee slammed the van into gear and started speeding away. Jake watched Harlan disappear in the mirror and smiled contentedly while Billy Thompson, who was seated between them, took another slug from a half-empty bottle of whisky and belched. "Do we gotta go back for that deer or did you miss another one?" he asked drunkenly.

"Give me that," grunted Jake as he snatched the bottle away from Billy. "You've had enough." He put the bottle to his face and took a long swallow. "You haven't done any better tonight, Billy, so don't be talking trash to me."

"Knock it off!" barked Ricky. "Both of you!" He made a quick left on an unmarked dirt road and pulled to the side. "Jake, you aren't shooting any more tonight; you had too much to drink. I want you to switch seats with Billy. It's his turn."

"But Billy had just as much as me," complained Jake.

"I don't want to hear it," snapped Ricky. "Just do what I said."

Jake unlatched the door, shoved it open with a shoulder, and promptly fell out of the van onto the grassy berm.

Ouff!

Ricky shook his head wearily. "Let's get him back inside," he said to Billy. "We haven't killed anything yet and time is getting short."

When Ricky and Billy slid out of the van to get Jake, he was lying motionless on the ground, and for a moment they thought he might be dead. But when Ricky stooped low to check his breathing, he heard him snoring softly. Ricky grabbed him by the collar and shook him hard. "Wake up, sleepy head!"

Jake sat bolt upright. "Am I bleeding?" he yelped, pawing at his head and chest clumsily.

"No," said Billy. "But you're gonna be if you say anything else about my shooting abilities."

And with that, Jake's eyes rolled back in his head and he began to snore once again.

"Come on," said Ricky. "Let's get him in the van."

Both men grabbed Jake by his armpits and helped him back into the vehicle, semi-conscious. Billy climbed into the passenger seat while Ricky slid behind the wheel. Ricky was losing patience with Jake and Billy. They were both wasted. Realizing the odds that either one of them could shoot straight were slim at best, he reached over and popped open the glovebox, pulling out a large bag of beef jerky. "Chow down girls," he said. "We're gonna be here for a couple hours until you both sober up." He looked at Billy. "There's a thermos of black coffee behind the seat. Help yourself. No more booze tonight."

It was six o'clock in the morning when Ricky was startled awake by coyotes howling in the woods just outside his open

21

window. He couldn't believe he'd fallen asleep, and he slammed his palm against the steering wheel when he realized that it would soon be dawn.

He looked at his two partners in crime. Both dead asleep—Jake with a line of drool running down the corner of his chin, Billy snoring like a wart hog in heat, his mouth wide open.

"Wake up!" he shouted. "We don't have much time before sunup."

Jake and Billy sat straight up in their seats.

"Where are we?" mumbled Jake, still groggy from too much whiskey.

"Hill Billy Junction for all I know," said Ricky. "We gotta get moving if we want to kill a deer before daylight."

Ricky switched on the ignition and dropped the van into gear. He was lost. Not sure which way to go, he started driving aimlessly, hoping to spot a deer on the way back to camp…wherever that was.

He soon came to a crossroad and turned right for no particular reason and continued on for several miles before spotting a small band of deer standing in a vacant field. There was a house nearby, but with his desire to kill something before sunrise, he threw caution to the wind and stopped at the edge of the field. "Okay, Billy," he said. "Try not to miss this time. If you do, we're heading back to camp empty handed."

Billy leaned out the passenger window with Ricky's 30-06 rifle pressed to his shoulder. There were five antlerless deer grazing in the open field right in front of him. With enough residual moonlight remaining for a clear view of the deer, Billy put the iron sights on the largest one, held his breath, and slowly squeezed the trigger.

The rifle barked once, shattering the still night air. Four of the deer ran off with their tails held high. The fifth one dropped dead in its tracks.

"Nice shot!" cheered Ricky. Then he swung his van into the field and raced toward the fallen deer.

Jason Smith was enjoying an early breakfast of scrambled eggs and bacon when he heard the gunshot. It sounded close, so he stood from the table, killed the overhead lights, and peered out the kitchen window. At first, he saw only the skeletons of naked oaks and maples under a predawn sky. But then there was a flash of red in a vacant field three hundred yards away.

Brake lights!

It had to be poachers; of that he was certain. Slipping into a pair of work boots and a heavy jacket, he ran out the front door into the brisk morning air and jumped into his pickup truck. In the distance, he saw the silhouette of a vehicle sitting in the field with its lights turned off. It looked like a van. Determined to stop them, Jason keyed the ignition and dropped his truck into gear. Turning onto the macadam road at the end of his driveway, he decked the accelerator and sped toward the van.

Billy was sitting in the passenger seat with the rifle barrel sticking up between his knees when he spotted Jason Smith's pickup truck coming toward them. He whipped his head toward Ricky. "We got company and they're coming fast!"

Ricky looked back toward the road. In the distance a pair of headlights loomed toward them. "Time to go!" he cried as he cranked the steering wheel and made a wide U-turn. He stepped on the gas and sped toward the road hoping to get ahead of the oncoming vehicle. The van pitched and bobbed across the uneven ground as they fled, unable to gain solid traction in the grassy field. For a moment, it looked like the approaching vehicle might reach them before they got away, but their tires suddenly bit into solid turf, propelling them onward.

Jason Smith slammed on his brakes and came to a gut wrenching stop as the van bounced onto the road directly in

23

front of him, its tires spewing clumps of brown sod on the macadam as they sped off.

He watched them go, realizing it was useless to give chase. And although they'd managed to get away, Jason got the license number off the bumper and quickly drove back to his house to call the game warden.

Deputy Swanson was sitting on an overlook watching for night shooters when the dispatcher radioed him about the incident. A Ford van with New York tags that matched the vehicle he was looking for. He wasn't surprised to learn that it was still out there. Encouraged that he would catch them this time, he started his engine and sped off in the direction of Smith's property.

Deputy Swanson had been cruising one lonely country road after another looking for the van as the sun slowly ascended in the east. After an hour or so, he began to give up hope when he spotted the vehicle parked alongside a rundown trailer tucked into a grove of pines on a back road to nowhere. Swanson parked behind the van, got out of his truck, and took a closer look. There were traces of blood and deer hair on the back bumper, and the hood was still warm to the touch, indicating it hadn't been there long. Knowing it was always better to have backup while investigating an active poaching case, he returned to his vehicle, grabbed the mic off the dash, and called the Game Commission's regional headquarters requesting Chuck's assistance.

After pounding on the door of the trailer with his fist several times, Chuck finally heard footsteps approaching. Somebody inside fumbled with the latch longer than necessary before the door squeaked open just enough to peek out at them. Chuck could smell the heavy stench of alcohol coming from inside as he slid his foot against the door so it couldn't close. He identified himself and Bill Swanson as state game wardens even though they were both in full uniform, then said: "I guess you know why we're here."

The man behind the door said nothing at first. He simply stepped back and opened it wide. Dressed only in his underwear, he was in his mid-twenties, stoop-shouldered, and thin as a rail with curly brown hair and eyes bloodshot from too much alcohol.

"This has gotta be about the deer," he said. "I was afraid you guys would show up." He looked back over his shoulder. "Jake, Billy, wake up! We got company."

Chuck watched as two other young men in the shadows of the trailer began to stir, one sleeping on a couch, the other on a mattress lying on the floor. Keeping a cautious eye on both, he asked the stoop-shouldered man for his name.

"I'm Ricky Lee," he answered, hugging himself with his arms. "Come on in. I ain't dressed and it's cold outside."

Chuck and his deputy stepped into the narrow trailer and watched as Ricky's two partners tossed their covers aside and sat up, both rubbing the sleep from their eyes.

The place was a mess. Not as bad as the House of Horrors without toilet facilities he'd been in earlier, but a mess just the same. Chuck waited while all three men put some clothes on. Once they were dressed, he asked Ricky to sign a written consent for them to search the trailer and the exterior premises. Ricky agreed without an argument. All three men seemed hung over from a hard night of drinking, and Chuck figured that was probably why they were so compliant. After checking their drivers' licenses, Chuck learned that they all lived two hundred miles away in Astoria, New York and had been in Pennsylvania for three days. They'd come a long way to wreak havoc on the deer in his district.

Chuck and his deputy searched the trailer and found nothing incriminating. From there, they moved to the van parked outside.

It reeked of alcohol. On the floor and seats were bottles of Southern Comfort whisky, empty beer cans, spent and loaded cartridge cases, deer hair and blood, bloody knives, and two

Browning rifles. The uncased rifles—a 30-06 and a .308—were seized and tagged as evidence along with the knives and samples of deer hair and blood. Judging from the number of empty cartridges in the van, they had done a lot of shooting in the last several days.

When they walked back behind the trailer, they found the skinned carcass of a doe hanging from the branch of an oak tree. Chuck asked Ricky who killed the deer.

"Jake did," he said.

"When?"

"Two days ago. He's a crack shot…that is until he starts sipping on the hard stuff like last night. Then it's over."

"How many deer did you guys kill last night?" asked Chuck. "Be honest and I'll take that into consideration when I write your citations. Now that it's daylight, we're going back to check the fields where you were spotted anyway."

"Just one," said Ricky. "Billy got that one. I was driving and Jake and Billy took turns shooting. They missed the others because they were drinking too much." He paused, then offered a lame half-shrug. "Guess I was too. I ain't gonna lie."

"Where is the deer Billy shot?" Chuck asked.

"Don't know. It lays back in a field somewhere. It was dark, and I'm not sure I could find the place again. We were looking for it when we saw headlights coming our way, so we skedaddled out of there."

Deputy Swanson told Chuck about his meeting with Jason Smith earlier and how Smith had heard a rifle shot near his house and chased after them. Swanson volunteered to go back and look for the deer. Chuck agreed. The odds of finding it were excellent now that the sun was up.

Chuck waited at the trailer with the three suspects in custody while Swanson drove back to the field where Jason Smith had spotted their van. He returned an hour later with a freshly killed doe in the bed of his pickup truck.

Since the men were non-residents, and there was no extradition law for crimes of this nature, Chuck had no choice but to transport them to the local district judge, Marjorie Wheaton, for an immediate hearing. If they failed to post bail, she would put them in jail until they came up with the money to pay their fines.

At Wheaton's office, twelve citations were filed against the three men with fines totaling twenty-four hundred dollars. Chuck kept the rifles, a spotlight, and some ammunition for evidence. He would have impounded the van too but they had no other way of getting back to Astoria, New York.

All three men pled guilty and made arrangements to pay their fines in full. When Ricky found out that both of his rifles would be confiscated, he asked if there was some way to get them back. Chuck explained that the Game Commission had an auction every year in Harrisburg for confiscated equipment (the practice was discontinued a few years later) and that he knew of people who had bid on their own confiscated firearms in order to get them back. Ricky thanked him for the information, a glimmer of hope in his eyes.

With the case finally resolved, Chuck and Bill Swanson left Judge Wheaton's office and drove out to their favorite restaurant for some breakfast and coffee. A hearty meal along with some conversation about the arrest helped bond their relationship and made the extended hours and dangers they faced seem less stressful than they actually were. Still, the day was just beginning, and both men knew that anything could happen, and usually did, during hunting season in Pennsylvania. What they didn't know was just how true that premise would turn out to be in the coming hours.

After finishing breakfast, Chuck and Deputy Bill Swanson parted company so Bill could dispose of the two illegal deer that they had confiscated. The deer that was skinned and gutted would go to a needy family, but the other had been fed on by coyotes and was spoiled. Swanson would dispose of that one by tossing it into a deer pit (a six-foot-deep trench, usually fifteen or twenty feet long, dug into the earth by a backhoe). Deer pits are located behind locked gates in remote sections of our State Game Lands that are open to the public for hunting, trapping, and fishing. The deer carcasses would be consumed by bears, coyotes, vultures, and other critters over time.

Chuck hadn't gone far when his mobile radio crackled to life. A dispatcher relayed a message from a Game Commission supervisor requesting his assistance at the scene of a poaching incident in northern Susquehanna County. The officer assigned to that district was on sick leave and unavailable.

Chuck responded immediately, and when he pulled onto the property thirty minutes later, he saw a state-issued sedan belonging to a regional supervisor and several other deputy vehicles parked in front of a shabby-looking wood-framed house. As he exited his patrol car, two supervisors approached and quickly brought him up to date on the incident.

There were five suspects on the property, including Alphonse Petrovick, a cocky braggart who claimed he owned the place. All of the suspects were in their early thirties and had been drinking and appeared to be mildly intoxicated. The deputies had discovered deer hair and blood that hadn't dried in the trunk of Petrovick's car and more hair and blood in the kitchen along with about thirty pounds of fresh venison that had been cut up.

The five men were nonresidents from New Jersey. They all admitted knowing about the deer and claimed it was a roadkill they had picked up. It was the same old excuse Chuck had heard a hundred times before, and he didn't believe them. But no matter how hard the supervisors and deputies had pressed them for the truth, none of the men would admit doing anything wrong.

The supervisors were looking for more evidence, something that would show that the deer wasn't a roadkill and instead had been killed by one of the suspects, but they couldn't find anything conclusive. They were in a quandary now and wanted a second opinion on what to do since neither of them had been involved in law enforcement for a number of years.

Chuck needed to look around a bit and familiarize himself with the situation before he could help them, so he went into the house to see what he could find. It was a single-story home with an A-frame roof. The exterior paint was peeling off the sides and the wilting roof was in desperate need of repair. The place was a filthy mess inside, just like the last two he'd been in today. The carpets hadn't been vacuumed in years. A ratty overstuffed couch and two wooden chairs sat in the center of the living room. A widescreen television was parked directly in front of the furniture. There were no beds, just rumpled sleeping bags tossed on the floor. He walked into the kitchen and found bloodstains on the Formica counter and traces of deer hair on the linoleum floor. When he checked the refrigerator, it was stocked with dozens of beer cans along with multiple packages of fresh venison that had been cut up and wrapped in cellophane.

Chuck walked back outside. Alphonse Petrovick was putting on a good show for his buddies, acting like a jerk and being belligerent to the officers present. He was playing the tough guy and looked the part. Lean and tall, he had a pinched face with piercing green eyes and a thick horseshoe mustache. He stood defiantly before the wardens with his hands on his hips as they questioned him. Oddly, he had a stuffed crow pinned to the shoulder of his checkered shirt and wore cut-off jeans and black high-top boots laced just below his knees as if playing the part of an early-century buccaneer with a parrot on his shoulder.

Since it wasn't Chuck's case or his district, he took a step back and tried to blend into the background as the supervisors attempted to question Petrovick and his cohorts about the deer. But after another thirty minutes had passed with no action taken against the suspects, Chuck finally decided to take charge of the situation, not knowing how the supervisors would react. As far as he was concerned, there was enough evidence to charge all of them with possessing parts of a whitetail deer unlawfully taken. Although bow season was open, none of them had archery licenses or archery equipment, which would bolster the case against them.

"All right, this is what we're going to do," Chuck said loud enough for everyone to hear. He looked directly at Petrovick. "We're going to do a body search on all five of you. Then we're going to handcuff you and transport you to the district judge in Montrose. You can tell him your story and see if he believes you."

Chuck assigned deputies to frisk and handcuff each suspect after reading their Miranda Warnings. Once they were mirandized and cuffed, their moods changed. They became more somber realizing that the wardens were serious and that they were facing possible jail time. Chuck told the deputies what charges he wanted filed against the men and had them prepare citations so that all he had to do was look over the paperwork and sign everything before they transported the men to court.

Before he left with the deputies and his prisoners, Chuck informed the supervisors that he wouldn't need them any longer. They hadn't witnessed anything and couldn't provide any testimony that would help him in court. Since they lived in outlying counties a considerable distance away, they didn't argue and began making their way home without saying much.

After everything was checked and any evidence such as deer hairs, blood samples, and the venison discovered in the house was gathered, Chuck and his men drove to Montrose with their prisoners held in several vehicles.

Because the men were nonresidents, and probably wouldn't respond to any citations issued to them on the scene, Chuck had no recourse but to transport them to Montrose for an immediate hearing. Chuck knew that if he left them go on their own recognizance there would be nothing he could do if they didn't respond to the citations except have arrest warrants issued. But he would only be able to serve the warrants if they came back to Pennsylvania and he happened to learn of it and then locate and apprehend them. Those odds were meek at best.

When the wardens pulled into the parking lot in front of the courthouse in Montrose (Susquehanna County Seat) they made an immediate impression on some of the local officials.

They were shocked and impressed when they witnessed the armed and uniformed game wardens unload five handcuffed, grubby looking men and then usher them into the courthouse. One of the attorneys who was there at the time, later commented to Chuck about the positive image that scene had portrayed to him.

Chuck escorted the men into the judge's chambers and there was an immediate hearing held. Chuck was sworn in and explained the case to the judge, after which the suspects had an opportunity to present arguments for their defense. Alphonse Petrovick was the only one to take the stand. He gave the judge the same phony story about the deer being a roadkill, but the judge didn't believe him and found him guilty of possessing an unlawfully killed deer. The other four men knew it was useless to tell the same story as Petrovick, so they all pled guilty rather than waste time with a lengthy hearing. Since they didn't have the money to pay their five-hundred-dollar fines, all five men were committed to the county jail, but not before they began arguing with each other and blaming each other for their predicament. As far as Chuck was concerned, they should have thought about that earlier before their heavy drinking overtook their common sense, if indeed they had any.

Chuck was proud of the way the deputies handled themselves and happy that the case had come to a successful conclusion. But it had also been lengthy and time consuming. It was late afternoon, and he wanted to get back into his own district and resume patrolling for the remainder of the day.

After sharing a quick coffee break with the deputies and commending them for their professional conduct throughout the investigation, they parted ways and he started heading back toward the southern end of the county. Chuck had only traveled a short distance when his radio squawked. It was another call from a Game Commission dispatcher. The message was bleak. The regional director wanted him to come to the office immediately for a discussion about the incident at the Petrovick property. Chuck couldn't help but wonder if the regional director (top boss) wanted to chew him out for taking charge of the case and dismissing the supervisors the way he had.

The late afternoon sun was an hour from dropping below the horizon as Chuck drove south on Route 29 toward the office. Chuck thought he might have ruffled some feathers with the two supervisors who had been there. If so, that would have been more than enough reason to set the director off. If that was the case, then so be it. Chuck was certain he'd done the right thing, and he decided to head directly to the office and meet his supervisor head-on rather than dream up some reason why he couldn't get there. That was the way Chuck rolled. He preferred to grab a bull by the horns and ride it out, win or lose, rather than walk away from a confrontation.

Life as a game warden in those days had more positives than negatives. Unlike today, there were no computers in state issued vehicles, no tracking devices so the boss knew where you were every minute of every day. No cell phones either. Everything was built on trust. When hunting season was open, you worked hard, sometimes day and night for months. You made your own hours, too. If a game warden was aware of night shooters working in a certain area, he'd work nights for a spell and would rest up during the day if he wanted to. If he put in an eighty-hour week and wanted to take a day off, the boss was okay with it. As long as you did your job and got your paperwork in on time, you were pretty much on your own. But it worked in reverse too. If the boss didn't like you, life as a game warden could be quite unpleasant in comparison with the freedom most other officers enjoyed.

Chuck didn't know what to expect when he walked through the front door of the regional office and saw the boss standing in the hallway in full uniform with his arms folded across his chest. There was no formal greeting. He looked him up and down briefly, then said, "Come back to my office; I have something to show you."

Chuck followed him down a long cinderblock hallway that served as a corridor for a half dozen small offices that housed the other gold badges that worked at regional headquarters: a law enforcement supervisor, a land management supervisor, a public relations supervisor, a wildlife specialist, and several others, not to mention a handful of secretaries and clerks.

The regional director's office was twice the size of the others, and it was at the very end of the hallway. The boss called over his shoulder for Chuck to close the door behind him as he walked in. Then he sat at his desk and motioned for Chuck to come forward. With his powerful build, stern face and eighteen-inch neck, he could be an intimidating figure. "I was briefed about the poaching incident in northern Susquehanna County earlier today," he said.

Chuck nodded, expecting the worst.

The director reached under his desk, pulled open a drawer, and withdrew a sheet of white copy paper with several typewritten paragraphs on one side. "I want you to know that I've written a letter of commendation about how you handled the case," said the director. "I'm going to forward it to the front office in Harrisburg and put it in your personal file."

Chuck was relieved to hear this. "I appreciate that," he said.

"Well, I appreciate it too," returned the director. "I want you to know that the letter states that I am especially proud to learn of your promptness and professionalism in answering a call for assistance. And not only you, but your deputies as well. The manner in which your deputies performed their duties in the arrest and court procedures is a direct reflection of your professionalism as a law enforcement officer."

"Thank you," said Chuck.

"I'm not done yet," said the director. "I also wrote that because of your concern for your brother officers a bad scene was likely prevented. And the way you managed the case was, in my opinion, a work of art in law enforcement procedures that resulted in the successful conviction of known Game Law violators."

"Thank you, again," said Chuck.

The director eyed him critically for a moment, then said, "In fact, you did such a fine job that I'm putting the northern district under your immediate jurisdiction for a while. It's been vacant too long and the locals know about it."

Chuck nodded that he understood.

"We've had a lot of night shooting up there lately," the director added. "We won't have a salaried officer back on duty for at least another week, and I'm counting on you to cover it for us until he returns."

"I'll do my best," said Chuck.

"I know you will."

The boss leaned back in his chair and motioned toward the door with his heavy chin. "I've taken enough of your time, Chuck. The day is almost over. You should head home and get some rest. Hate to say it, but I wouldn't be surprised if you have to go back up there again tonight."

Later that evening, long after Chuck had finished dinner and settled in for the night with his wife and two daughters, he received a call from a dispatcher about a deputy who was requesting his assistance. The deputy was following a pickup truck and had his headlights turned off so they couldn't see him. There were two men in the cab and another standing in the bed shining a spotlight into some fields. The truck was creeping along a winding township road, and the deputy suspected they were going to shoot a deer. Chuck instructed the dispatcher to have his deputy continue following the truck for as long as he could and said that he would be there shortly.

Chuck jumped into his uniform, strapped on his .357 magnum revolver, and climbed into his patrol car. He would be there in minutes. The location the dispatcher had given him was close by. Most calls about spotlighting and night shooting turned out to be miles away, sometimes at the far end of his district, and he would know before hanging up the phone that the odds of catching them would be slim at best. But now, with his deputy following the truck, combined with its close proximity, the odds were in his favor.

The night had turned colder with a heavy cloud cover that concealed the moon. Chuck drove as fast as he could on the dark and narrow highway hoping to reach his deputy before any trouble started when his radio came alive.

"They're running!" called the deputy. "They must have spotted us; we're going to chase them." His voice betrayed the adrenalin pumping through his veins as the pursuit began.

Chuck realized at once that his deputy had a partner along with him (*we're going to chase them*) and was relieved he wasn't alone. He listened on his mobile radio as the deputies repeated their locations while pursuing the speeding pickup truck. Several other deputies homed in on the conversation trying to determine which way the vehicle was headed so they could intercept it, but the truck was driving at a terribly high rate of speed and managed to lose them all.

Chuck and his men began to search the area, the deputies heading north while Chuck drove in a southerly direction. Their persistence soon paid off when the deputies spotted the pickup in the parking lot of the Raunchy Tavern, a place of ill repute not far into a neighboring county that was outside of Chuck's district.

When Chuck pulled into the parking lot, his two deputies were standing by a red Ford pickup truck and waved him over. The lot was packed with vehicles, mostly other pickup trucks belonging to local hunters. Chuck parked behind the red Ford and got out of his patrol car.

"You sure this is the right one?" he asked as he approached his deputies.

They were positive right down to the license plate they had copied when they first spotted the vehicle. There was nobody in the truck, nor was anyone in the parking lot, which meant the occupants were most likely inside the bar unless they had run off somewhere. Chuck wasn't about to go searching for them in the dark without a strong indication that they'd fled on foot, and he didn't want to wait in the parking lot until they walked out of the bar, especially after they'd been drinking.

The place closed at two o'clock in the morning; they could be there for hours. The only option was to go inside and try to find them.

The bar was a one-story rectangular wooden structure with a tall A-frame roof exhibiting a large neon sign glowing with green, orange, and red letters displaying THE RAUNCHY TAVERN for all the world to see. There were two windows in the front of the building, both covered with iron grates designed to prevent thieves from breaking into the place after hours. The only entry was through a single commercial-grade steel deer, also designed to keep crooks out when the bar was closed.

Everyone turned their heads when three uniformed game wardens strolled into the dimly lit bar through a haze of cigarette smoke that hung in the air like swamp fog. The place smelled of stale beer and spilled liquor, and the cheap tile floor stuck to the soles of their boots as they walked to the center of the bar. The patrons stared briefly with uncomprehending eyes, then turned back to their drinking and boasting, pretending to ignore the officers. They were an odd sight indeed for a place packed with dedicated drinkers, many of whom had never seen a game warden before in their lives.

A bearish man with a bristly beard seated at a dimly lit back table yelled, "Hey Rex, better hide that deer you shot last night!" The other three men seated with him snorted and guffawed at his wisecrack. Chuck and his deputies ignored them.

"We're looking for the owner of a red Ford pickup truck parked outside," announced Chuck loud enough for all to hear. There was little response with the exception of a few drunken mumblings. "Last call!" Chuck quickly added. "I'm going to send for a tow truck and impound the vehicle for evidence if no one claims it."

A sudden hush came over the bar as the men set down their drinks and looked about the room, waiting for someone to answer back.

A young man in his early twenties finally spoke up: "I drove the truck," he called out as he slipped off a bar stool and approached. He was clean shaven with soft eyes, a full face, and stylish hair parted on one side and combed back.

The same bearish man from the back table shouted that it looked like the rabbit cops got their man, generating a short burst of laughter from his intoxicated friends. The wardens stayed focused on their case at hand and continued to pay him no mind.

Chuck knew he couldn't question the suspect inside of a crowded bar, so he escorted him out the front door and into the parking lot along with his deputies. Chuck was glad to be out of the place and filled his lungs with fresh air as they approached the red Ford pickup.

"What's your name?" asked Chuck.

"Gerry Raye."

"Any firearms inside your truck?"

"No. You're welcome to look for yourself. It's unlocked."

"Then why did you run when you spotted my deputies?" asked Chuck.

Gerry shrugged and looked away. "I don't know," he said. "Scared, I guess."

While his deputies searched the truck for evidence, Chuck asked Gerry for identification and he pulled a wallet from his back pocket, extracted a driver's license from inside, and handed it to him. Chuck took a pen and notepad from his back pocket and wrote down the information he'd need for a citation.

"Who were the other two with you tonight?" asked Chuck.

"I was alone," said Gerry. "Nobody was in the truck but me."

"Don't lie to me," cautioned Chuck. "We know you had two friends with you. One was standing in the back of the truck shining a spotlight into the fields."

Gerry dropped his chin and said nothing.

As Chuck was about to question him further, one of his deputies called him over to the back of the truck.

"We found a bag of marijuana under the driver's seat," the deputy told him. "No guns, blood, or hair anywhere. Other than the weed, there's nothing. Spotlight is gone too."

"They must have hidden it somewhere after they lost us," said Chuck. "If they had any firearms, they probably got rid of them too. Could be anywhere."

Chuck walked back to Gerry Raye and told him about the marijuana they found.

"I didn't put it there," claimed Gerry. "I don't know anything about it."

"Doesn't matter," said Chuck. "It's in your truck, which means you can be arrested for possession of an illegal substance."

"That don't seem fair."

"Fair or not, it's the law," said Chuck. "Besides, your truck reeks with the smell of skunkweed. You had to know it was there."

Gerry stuffed his hands in his pockets and stared down at his boots. "You gonna arrest me?"

"Depends on how much you cooperate from this point on," Chuck told him. "I want the names and addresses of the other two who were with you."

Gerry considered his options for a moment, then said, "Okay, but only if you forget about the weed you found."

"No promises," said Chuck. "But it would be to your advantage to cooperate."

Gerry blew a heavy sigh. "Just don't tell them it was me who told you, okay?"

As Gerry Raye finished giving Chuck the information he needed, the front door of the Raunchy Tavern burst open, and a crowd of unruly customers filed into the parking lot. Chuck didn't know if the other two suspects were part of the group, but suspected they probably were.

There were a dozen or more men, most of them in their twenties and thirties, all of them had been drinking heavily. They immediately started shouting profanities at Chuck and his deputies, becoming increasingly more vocal by the second. Chuck had all the information he needed in order to file citations on all three suspects at that point and saw no need to remain in the parking lot while a bunch of drunks hurled insults at him and his deputies. He signaled for his men to follow him, and they left the area.

Chuck and his deputies stopped at a coffee shop once they got back into Susquehanna County to discuss the case. One of his deputies was familiar with Gerry Raye and told Chuck he lived at home and that his mother worked at a woman's state prison in in the neighboring county. Hoping she might be on duty, Chuck used a phone in the back of the coffee shop to call the prison and asked for her. As luck would have it, Mrs. Raye was working nights and agreed to speak with him. After briefing her about the case and the marijuana they found, he gave her the names of the other two young men involved with her son and asked if she knew them and could verify the information her son had given him regarding their home addresses.

"I know who they are, all right," she said. "They're always hanging out at that disgusting bar with my Gerry. He wouldn't have been there at all if it weren't for those two miscreants."

Chuck said, "I'm not too concerned about the marijuana we found, but I do want to know if they had guns in the truck. We're sure they hid them somewhere before they got to the bar. If you can get your son to tell the truth about the firearms, I'll forget about the loco weed they had in the truck."

She paused for a moment, then said. "You might forget about it, but I sure won't. Don't you worry, officer, I'll be off shift in an hour. I'll talk to Gerry about this as soon as he comes home. Where can I reach you?"

Chuck gave her the phone number of the regional office. "I'll be working for a few more hours tonight," he said. "Call if you learn anything. A dispatcher will contact me, and I'll get back to you."

"You can count on it, officer. And I apologize for my son's behavior tonight."

When Chuck's mobile radio crackled with an incoming call at midnight, he was parked atop an overlook watching the farmland below for late spotlighters. The dispatcher told him that he had a message from Mrs. Raye stating that she had the information he wanted, and to call her right away.

Chuck started his engine, backed away from the ledge onto a narrow country lane, and drove into Montrose where he knew of a phone booth at a gas station that he could use to make a call. Stepping inside the accordion doors, he closed them and dialed the phone number the dispatcher had provided. It rang once. "Is this Officer Arcovitch?" asked Mrs. Raye.

"Yes," he answered. "Thanks for getting back to me."

"Oh, you're very welcome, officer. I spoke with my son just now. He's sitting here right beside me, and he wants to talk to you."

"Put him on."

Chuck could hear a murmur of voices in the background. It sounded like Gerry and his mother were bickering over whether or not he would talk. After a moment, Gerry spoke into the phone. "Hello?" he said timidly.

"Gerry, this is Officer Arcovitch. I understand you have something you want to tell me."

There was a long pause. Then: "Um...well, I guess so."

"I'm listening," said Chuck.

After another long pause, Gerry Raye finally gave Chuck a complete confession. He told him that his two friends ran out the back door of the bar when Chuck and his deputies walked inside, and that they hitchhiked back to their homes. He admitted having a rifle in the truck at the time they were spotlighting deer and agreed to plead guilty to the Game Law violation. He said his two friends live at home, just like he does, and that his mother had already called their parents and told them to expect a visit from the game warden.

"Where is the rifle and spotlight," asked Chuck. "It wasn't in your truck when we searched it."

"We hid them in the woods after we lost you. I went back and got them on my way home tonight. They're here at the house."

When Chuck was finished with Gerry, he asked for his mother to come to the phone. He thanked her for her help and told her that citations would be coming in the mail and that the fines would be five hundred dollars for her son as well as his two friends. He made arrangements to stop by the house and pick up the rifle and spotlight for evidence the following day and promised not to charge any of them with the marijuana violation since it looked like the case would be settled.

"I'll make sure Gerry pays his fine, officer," she said. "And he isn't getting off scot-free for the marijuana either. He knows he has rules to follow as long as he lives here with me. I'll be taking care of that problem in my own way."

By the sound of her voice, Chuck had no doubt she meant it, too.

With the case apparently resolved, Chuck returned to his hiding place on a remote hilltop overlooking several thousand acres of cropland crisscrossed by three county roads. Another vehicle with two deputies inside was strategically hidden along a narrow lane that led into the woods several hundred yards below him. It was well after midnight. Spotlighting wildlife was illegal at this time, and the deputies would be in position to pursue anyone shining a light or taking a shot at a deer while Chuck watched from above. He'd been getting reports of night shooting in the area and hoped to put an end to the poaching activity.

Chuck realized that sitting out on night patrol was usually fruitless. Even when you could see spotlights working and hear occasional shots, most times you couldn't locate the shooters before they were gone unless you were right on top of them. Chuck often thought he was better off sitting at home waiting for the phone to ring with a caller giving good information on a violation in progress. Over the years, a good phone tip produced far more cases than sitting out in the middle of nowhere hoping a poacher would shoot a deer right in front of you. With a district that covered four hundred square miles, what were the odds?

But tonight would prove differently, for he hadn't been sitting for more than thirty minutes when the arc of a spotlight flashed across the black sky. Chuck grabbed his binoculars from the passenger seat and scanned the fields below. He could see an intense yellow beam sweeping the distant fields long before he saw the vehicle. It was around a bend in the road and too far off as it slowly came toward the deputies. Chuck radioed his men and told them to get ready. Tucked back in the woods as they were, they couldn't see the beam from the approaching spotlighter even though the vehicle would soon be driving right past their hiding spot.

Soon a Buick station wagon with its headlights turned off came around the bend in full view of Chuck. He waited. There were no deer or any wildlife in the spotlight as they lit up the fields. Technically, it was only a late spotlighting violation. A complication of the law as written kept him frozen in place, waiting to see if they'd locate a deer so he could have his men swoop in on them.

The vehicle continued past his deputies, then turned right at a curve in the road and drove down into a hollow. He could see their light arcing across the sky as they searched, but he didn't have a view of their vehicle because they were too far into the hollow and completely out of sight. When their beam stopped moving and remained steady, Chuck was certain they had a deer captured in the light. He could sense it. He leaned closer to the open window and listened for the rifle shot that would come next.

BOOM!

The shot rang through the valley below, shattering the still night air. Seconds later, the station wagon turned on its headlights and came back out of the hollow moving fast, heading directly toward his deputies parked back in the woods.

Chuck grabbed his microphone off the dashboard. "They're heading right for you," he said into the mic. "Stop them!"

"They just shot right past us," a deputy radioed back. "Do you want us to go after them?"

Chuck paused, considering what to do for a moment. Then: "No, stay where you are," he said. "Let's see if they come back."

Although Chuck didn't know if they had killed a deer, he had a strong hunch that if they did shoot one, they would soon return for it. He knew that some poachers operated in this manner, hoping to evade any landowner or game warden that might be in the area. It would be a much stronger case if they caught them attempting to take possession of the deer rather than stop them a mile down the road empty-handed.

Thirty minutes passed when Chuck spotted the headlights of a vehicle coming toward his deputies again. He couldn't tell if it was the suspect's car at first, it was too far away, but he alerted his deputies by radio to be prepared. When the vehicle cruised slowly past their hiding spot, Chuck radioed them again and said that it was the same car as before, a Buick station wagon, and instructed them to follow it with their headlights off so they wouldn't be seen. Chuck stood by while his deputies tailed the vehicle. The deputies were only a few car lengths away when the Buick turned into the hollow and pulled to the edge of the road and stopped.

Seconds later, Chuck's radio came to life: "Driver's door just opened," a Deputy reported. "Looks like they're getting out of the car."

"Ten-four," answered Chuck. "I'm moving in now."

The wardens had them blocked in before they knew what happened. Chuck's emergency lights flashed bright red across the roof of his patrol car while his headlights illuminated the suspects' vehicle.

There were five men seated in the Buick as Chuck approached on foot with his flashlight trained on the driver. "State officers!" he declared. "Do you have any firearms in the vehicle?"

"No, sir," the man behind the wheel answered.

Chuck said, "Someone fired a shot from this car earlier. I want everyone to step out."

The men complied and Chuck had his deputies take them aside and frisk them for weapons while he searched the station wagon for firearms.

He looked in all the obvious places: under the seats, inside the spare tire well, the glove compartment, the console, but found nothing incriminating. There was no spotlight, no guns, no hair or blood. He crawled under the vehicle with his flashlight and searched diligently. Still no guns. He knew that many poachers were clever when it came to hiding firearms, but Chuck had checked everything and couldn't find so much as a spent cartridge case.

Next, Chuck sent one of his deputies into the field to search for a deer carcass. The deputy didn't go far before he came upon a freshly killed doe at the edge of a cornfield. It was still warm and obviously shot by the band of poachers they had in custody. Although Chuck had a fairly good case of circumstantial evidence (circumstantial evidence doesn't prove guilt but offers sound reasoning that a crime exists and requires additional evidence in order to support the claim), he would need more proof to get a conviction in court. With that in mind, he had his deputies write down the necessary information on notepads for a court trial while he took another look at their vehicle.

Chuck opened the rear passenger door and crawled inside the station wagon with his flashlight in hand. After searching the car's oversized rear storage area, he found deer hairs on the carpeted flooring. It wasn't much, just a few hairs, but it was enough to get their attention.

He climbed back out of the vehicle and turned to the men. "Listen up, all of you," he said. "I found some fresh deer hair in your car. We also know that you shot the doe that my deputy just found, so I don't care if it takes three days, we're going to everyone's house to search it until we get this straightened out."

It was two o'clock in the morning, and it looked like it was going to be a difficult case to crack. The leader of the group, whose name was Rodney, obviously had the other men under his power and he refused to talk. Chuck was determined to unravel this case, so he and his deputies got everyone back in their station wagon and escorted them to the nearest home twenty miles away and well into another neighboring officer's district. The deputy vehicle was in the lead as the three vehicles traveled in a motorcade with the suspects' car following directly behind it and Chuck's patrol car at the rear. If they broke away, he would light them up and chase them down.

The house was a rental tucked into a grove of oaks along a seldom used country road. Although not as bad as the other homes he'd been to earlier today, the place was dirty, cluttered, and in general reflected the character of its occupants.

While his deputies guarded the other three men, Chuck obtained permission to search from the two suspects who lived there and escorted them into the kitchen where he found a number of sharp cutting utensils strewn across the counter. Upon a closer look, he observed traces of muscle tissue and blood on several of the knives and temporarily secured them inside a drawer. Next, he opened the refrigerator and found a freshly wrapped venison tenderloin inside. There was little else.

"Where did the deer meat come from?" Chuck asked.

"I got it in season," one suspect said. "It's legal."

Chuck believed it was a lie, but since bow season was open, he asked him for his archery license to see if he'd removed the deer tag.

The man pretended to look around for it, opening drawers and checking coat pockets in a hall closet. Finally, he turned to Chuck and shrugged. "I guess I lost it," he said.

They always have an answer, thought Chuck. Just not the right one.

At that moment, one of Chuck's deputies burst into the house. "You gotta come outside and see this!" he said breathlessly. "We found deer parts everywhere!"

After a search of the house and the surrounding acreage had been completed, they had proof that at least thirteen deer had been brought into the property and processed for consumption by the five men they had under arrest. Chuck and his deputies immediately began the long process of collecting all of the incriminating evidence and labeling every piece of it. Dozens of photographs were taken, hides counted, tagged, and collected along with any deer antlers they found lying about the property. All of these items would be transported to the regional headquarters for storage in a walk-in freezer. Firearms, knives, cutting utensils, venison pieces, and other items were put into evidence bags to be stored for safe keeping in the event of a long and drawn-out hearing if the poachers decided to hire an attorney for their defense.

Because Chuck had been working in two neighboring districts as well as his own, he would contact the wardens assigned to the other two districts and inform them about what he had found. They, in turn, would be able to file some of the charges against the men along with him. Due to the large number of deer that had been processed, Chuck suspected the five poachers had been selling the venison on the black market. Unfortunately, there was no way he could prove it unless one of them admitted to the crime. Unlikely at best.

With all the evidence finally documented, Chuck planned to file charges against four of the five men. The other, a teenager, would receive a written warning. And because they had cooperated in the end, he didn't plan to stack every possible charge against them. Had their attitudes been hostile, their penalties would have been severe. Still, the fines would soar well into the thousands of dollars considering the number of deer they'd killed.

It had been a long passage into night, and dawn was breaking by the time they finished. Chuck had been on duty for more than twenty-four hours. It wasn't the first time, nor would it be the last that he would work straight through, day and night, during the course of his long career as a state game warden.

Chuck felt gratified with the case against Rodney and his cohorts. Although he couldn't prove it, he believed he had put an end to a poaching ring that had been selling venison from their unlawful kills. It had been a lot of hard work, not only for him, but for the deputies who assisted him with this complicated case.

For most game wardens, the reward for working day and night to catch poachers is the satisfaction they feel in return for hunting down and bringing to justice the outlaws who plunder our natural resources. And to State Game Warden Chuck Arcovitch and his dedicated deputies, it was worth every minute of it.

Chucked summed up his feelings about the job quite well in his book *A Conservation Officers Portfolio.* In his dedication page he wrote the following: "Game Warden, Game Protector, Wildlife Management Officer, Wildlife Conservation Officer, whatever the name the men and women who protect and conserve our wildlife resources are called, they are a unique breed. Few in number, the territory they cover is huge and the responsibilities they have are tremendous. They work all hours of the day and night. They face danger frequently and usually think little of it. They are often criticized for what they do, or for what they do not do. Most of the non-hunting public has no idea of what their job entails or how dangerous it can be. To others, like some members of the hunting fraternity, the game warden would give his own mother a ticket.

"Conservation officers [game wardens] are individuals who are extremely independent and opinionated, yet there is a team spirit that binds them together. Their love for our wildlife resources is only overshadowed by their unwritten code of honor and their steadfast devotion to duty. The danger and inconvenience they endure is a tradeoff for the freedom this profession offers them. Often, they teasingly criticize one another, but never do they ignore a brother officer's call for help, on or off the job. They are innovators constantly looking for new and better ways to do things. They truly are the thin green line that protects our wildlife resources from those who would destroy them if left alone.

"From its inception in 1895, the Pennsylvania Game Commission has produced hundreds of officers who have devoted their lives, and some who have given them, to their sworn duty of defending the commonwealth's wildlife resources. Being a game warden is not a job, it is a way of life! To my fellow brother and sister officers, living and deceased, not only in Pennsylvania but throughout the world, who 'walk the walk and talk the talk' of the conservation officer, I dedicate my book."

It's been a hard day's night
And I've been workin' like a dog
It's been a hard day's night
I should be sleepin' like a log
~Song by the Beatles

A HARD DAY'S NIGHT

DEPUTY MARSHALL STOVER almost missed the hunter dressed in camouflage while walking along the bank of the Susquehanna River that cold and dreary October evening. He wasn't sure what made him turn around and drive back. Something just didn't look right. Perhaps it was the way the man carried himself, the way he glanced over at the deputy's vehicle as it passed and then quickly turned his head away. That, in itself, proved nothing of course, but something clicked inside the deputy. Some inexplicable, profound, instinctive impulse deep inside of him said, *turn around.* And so, he did.

Darkness was setting in fast, and visibility was poor as he swung off the state road and wheeled down a wide concrete boat ramp toward the river. There were two men by the water dressed in camo hunting gear. One was the man he'd seen moments before, the other a much larger man of perhaps two hundred and fifty pounds who was carrying a medium-sized canvas tote bag that bulged at the sides. A small aluminum duck boat hitched to a trailer attached to a Jeep Wagoneer stood at the bottom of the ramp.

Stover parked his vehicle and climbed out. He was in full uniform including his badged green Stetson and marked waterproof patrol coat. Duck season was open, and he assumed the canvas tote bag contained a number of gamebirds.

"How was the hunting today?" he asked the men.

The big man shrugged. "Okay, I guess."

"I'm with the Pennsylvania Game Commission," said Stover as he walked over to him. "I'd like to take a look inside your game bag."

"Help yourself," the man replied. He dropped the bag at Stover's feet and stepped back.

The other man watched nervously as the deputy pulled a small Maglite from his coat pocket and knelt down and opened the zip-top canvas tote. Reaching inside, he pulled out five wood ducks and laid them on the concrete boat ramp side by side.

"The daily limit is two wood ducks," he said to the big man. "You have five."

"But I only killed two of them," he claimed. He nodded toward his partner. "Ben over there killed two and Brian killed the other one. We're waiting for him now. He should be along soon."

Stover explained that because the man was in possession of all five ducks, he was liable for a substantial penalty. Waterfowl regulations require that hunters do not leave any migratory game birds at any place or in the custody of another person unless the birds are tagged. Tags are supposed to include the hunter's signature, address, total number of birds taken and the date they were killed. None of the wood ducks had been tagged; thus, anyone in possession of the birds would be in violation, and the penalties are stiff.

Stover turned to Ben. "Did you kill two of these ducks?" he asked.

"Yes," he said. "But we don't have over the limit or anything like that. They're legal birds. We didn't know they had to be tagged. They're not deer; they're just ducks! What's the big deal?"

Stover ignored the question and proceeded to check their hunting licenses as well as their shotguns to be sure they were plugged to a three-round capacity. Then he used his handheld radio to call me. More hunters were bringing in boats and he wanted backup.

I was driving along a high-banked narrow hardtop road on my way to assist Deputy Stover when I spotted a deer from the corner of my eye as it leaped off the bank on my right in an attempt to clear my patrol car. It happened so fast that I had no time to react. There was a heavy thud as it hit the rooftop, missing my windshield by inches before sliding off the car onto the hard macadam road. Had I been traveling a little slower, the hundred-pound animal would have probably gone through my windshield, which could have resulted in severe injury to me or even my death.

I pulled to the shoulder and parked. Drawing a five-cell flashlight from between my seat and the console, I exited my Ford Bronco and walked over to the deer as it lay thrashing on the cold blacktop. It was a doe, and her back had been broken from the fall.

As I drew my revolver from its leather holster to end the animal's suffering, I heard approaching footfalls crunching through the leaves on the wooded embankment above. Expecting to see several more deer, I shined my flashlight into the trees and saw two dogs trotting toward me, both medium-sized mixed breeds. My mood suddenly turned dark, realizing that these free roaming dogs could have gotten me killed. Both wore collars, so I tried calling them to me, hoping to capture at least one, but they turned and ran off into the night. I got a good look at both and planned to return the following morning to see if I could locate them.

After dispatching the deer, I dragged its limp carcass over to my Bronco and loaded it onto the aluminum big game rack attached to the rear bumper. As I continued on to meet my deputy, I couldn't help but think about what had just happened.

I had always suspected that dogs were the cause of far more deer/vehicle collisions than they were blamed for. I realized that on occasion a dog will jump a fence or bolt out the front door even in the best of circumstances, but I also knew that many people allowed their dogs to run loose without ever considering the consequences.

Most free roaming dogs will chase wildlife; after all, they are predators at heart. Not only is that a violation of our state dog laws but it can also result in a heavy fine from the Game Commission. Additionally, dogs that are in the act of attacking big game can legally be killed in Pennsylvania by anyone witnessing the act.

It was October and the rutting season for deer had started and would run through November. I knew that these big game animals were more active at this time of year than at any other, and that Pennsylvania would have more deer killed by motor vehicles during October and November than at any other time (motorists should be particularly careful while driving during these two months but that doesn't mean you can ever let your guard down, as deer are struck during every month of the year). I recalled an incident years earlier where five deer seemed to magically appear in the center of the road directly in front of my car one night. I slammed my brakes and blew my horn, and they vanished as fast as they had appeared seconds before. I was certain my horn had triggered the reaction. A lesson learned that I never forgot.

State records showed that between forty thousand and fifty thousand deer are killed on our highways in Pennsylvania each year (1990s). I was certain that a significant number of these deer were surely chased onto the highways by dogs just as the doe that almost went through my windshield minutes earlier.

And it was with those thoughts fresh in my mind that I drove toward the river under a blackened sky, watching for the glowing yellow eyes of any deer that might be caught in my headlights.

As I eased my Bronco down the launch ramp to the Susquehanna River and parked, my uniformed deputy and his two suspects stood by the water's edge as a hunter dressed in camouflage docked his boat and walked over to meet them.

"Any luck?" Stover asked the hunter.

He looked over at my marked vehicle as I climbed out, then back to the deputy. "Is there a problem here, officer?"

"We have an issue with some untagged ducks," said Stover shining his flashlight on the five birds he'd lined up on the boat ramp earlier. "Are you Brian?"

"Yes."

"I was told one of them is yours."

Brian glanced down at the five wood ducks. "Nope. Mine are all in my boat," he said. "I don't know anything about those ducks."

Stover stepped over to Brian's boat and shined his flashlight into the bow. There were four wood ducks and three mergansers lying in a pile.

"You're over the limit," said Stover, walking back to the hunter. "Two woodies too many."

Brian's lips tugged into a frown. "I thought it was six per day."

"That's for mergansers, not wood ducks," Stover explained. "You need to spend more time studying the hunting rules and bag limits before you start shooting. All of that information is in the digest that comes with your hunting license."

Brian shook his head wearily and watched as Stover removed the two illegal wood ducks from his boat and put them in his car along with the five woodies he'd lined up on the ramp. After checking Brian's hunting license and verifying his identification, Stover wrote a citation for his two illegal ducks and handed it to him. Brian examined the citation and stuffed it into the back pocket without another word.

Stover followed up by writing another citation for three wood ducks over the limit and handed it to the big man.

"But I didn't kill those three ducks," he insisted. "Ben killed two of them. He even admitted it."

"How can you expect me to believe you?" asked Stover. "You told me that Brian killed one of the ducks, and he denied it. He wasn't with you when I drove in here either. It was just you and Ben. All I know is that you were in possession of five untagged wood ducks; that's three over the limit. I'm going to lock them in our storage freezer so you can have your day in court if you want. If the judge finds you not guilty, I'll return them to you."

"Yeah, right," the big man scoffed. "Here we are in Hillbilly Central, and you're probably friends with the judge. I'll just pay the fine and hunt somewhere else from now on."

Ben glanced over his shoulder at the river and said, "Look, it's getting late, officer. You got what you came for. Can we just go now?"

Stover noted a sense of urgency in Ben's voice, and that same instinctive impulse that had made him turn his vehicle around earlier told him that there was more to be found.

But he had inspected the men, their guns, licenses, game pouches and bags. What else could it be?

Suddenly it came to him: Ben's duck boat. He never checked it. Stover walked over to the boat and shined his flashlight into the decking for a quick look while I stood at the ramp with the three hunters. Centered between the seats, fore and aft, was a medium-sized Styrofoam cooler. Stover reached into the boat and removed the lid from the cooler to find that it was half full of unopened beer cans. Relieved to see it didn't contain any more illegal waterfowl, he closed the lid and started back toward us, scanning the area with his flashlight along the way.

I watched as he stopped suddenly, his flashlight trained on a weedy area alongside the ramp. Then he walked over and picked an empty beer can off the ground.

"Does this belong to anyone?" he called out, holding the can in the air.

All three hunters shook their heads no.

Because it was the same brand of beer that he found in Ben's cooler, Stover started working his flashlight along the riverbank and soon picked up another half dozen cans that had been strewn about the area. After checking the code numbers stamped on the bottom of the cans, he was able to confirm that they matched the cans inside Ben's cooler (beer manufacturers imprint an expiration date and batch code on all beer bottles and cans sold to consumers). With the evidence in hand, Stover wrote a citation for littering and handed it to Ben. He suspected the big man was also responsible for some of the littering but couldn't prove it so there was no citation filed in his case.

While Stover cleared everything up and secured the illegal ducks and empty cans for evidence, I did a little more scouting and found the remains of a freshly killed antlerless deer lying on the bank a short distance downstream. It had been boned out, and I could tell by the entry wound in the hide that it had been killed by an arrow. I suspected that whoever had dumped the carcass would be after another deer, and I made arrangements with Stover for the two of us to split up and patrol the surrounding area in the morning. With any luck, we might catch up with whoever was responsible for the illegal kill.

On my way home for the night, I got a radio call from the local fish warden asking if I could meet him. He was working along the Susquehanna River near Tunkhannock and had encountered a group of individuals who were drinking and partying along the bank. I started in that direction and radioed back advising him that I'd be at the Tunkhannock boat launch in twenty minutes.

In Pennsylvania (unlike all other states), fish and game are two completely separate agencies, each funded primarily by either fishing licenses or hunting licenses respectively. As a result, the fish wardens (called waterways conservation officers) work completely detached from their neighboring game wardens with neither lawman knowing what the other is up to on a daily basis. In this case, I had no idea my counterpart in conservation was only a dozen miles away working along the same stretch of the Susquehanna River as I had been until he contacted me by radio.

Pennsylvania game wardens and fish wardens both have police powers and can arrest people who've committed violations covered in the state's Crimes Code. For instance, someone under the influence of drugs or alcohol can be handcuffed and hauled off to jail by any salaried officer working for either agency. Don't get me wrong, I rarely see an intoxicated sport hunter. In all my years, I've only arrested one. Game wardens, however, find that poachers, especially those hunting deer at night with spotlights, are often under the influence of drugs, alcohol, or both. Because we spend untold hours behind the wheel of a patrol car, we also occasionally become involved with DUI cases (motorists driving under the influence of alcohol or drugs).

Underage drinking and BUI cases (boating under the influence) are violations fish wardens might come across. In fact, fish wardens are far more likely to find people who are fishing and boating while under the influence of drugs or alcohol than game wardens will ever find hunting under those circumstances.

Unfortunately, a few beers aren't always enough for some folks, and that's where the trouble begins. And so, when the local fish warden set out to patrol the Susquehanna River that evening, it came as no surprise that he encountered a group of people who were underage and drinking to excess, which was why I was on my way to Tunkhannock to meet with him.

My fellow officer was waiting along the Tunkhannock Park Boat Launch when I pulled in and parked. We shook hands and I listened while he briefed me on the situation. Shortly before dark, he observed a man and a woman fishing along the river while drinking bottles of beer. Both appeared to be in their mid-forties. He stayed back and watched from a short distance away. They seemed harmless enough and didn't know anyone was behind them. Both had fishing rods in their hands and were casting into the river and reeling their lines back in with bass lures attached. Although the man was properly licensed, his female companion didn't have a fishing license displayed so the warden started walking down the bank toward them. The woman heard him coming and quickly dropped her fishing rod on the ground. She was short and squat with a jowly face and suspicious brown eyes that darted about as if searching for a lost pet. When he asked to see her license, she claimed she wasn't fishing and that both fishing rods were her husband's. The warden told her he had been watching her for some time and held a different opinion. She shrugged, smiled briefly, and admitted casting her line into the river earlier. The woman agreed to pay her fine through a field citation and promised to have a check in the mail within a few days. Both she and her husband were cordial and polite.

As he continued upstream on foot, he spotted a huge bonfire burning along the riverbank. By now the sun had set, and a sizable number of people were gathered around the fire while drinking beer. The warden circled up the bank and into the woods where he had a better view of the group and would be out of sight. There were eight young people in all, and he thought some of them appeared to be in their teens. Rather than confront them alone, he walked back to the Tunkhannock boat launch and radioed out to me for assistance.

We were about to walk in on the party when the fish warden saw the same couple he had encountered fishing earlier. They were walking along the bank toward the gathering. Both were drinking bottles of beer and the woman was carrying a plastic garbage bag that appeared to be half full.

We stepped back into the woods and watched in the dark as they walked into the crowd. "Look out for the fish warden," she warned everyone. "He'll give you a ticket even if you only cast your line once."

"Is he coming here?" someone asked.

"Nah," she said. "He would've been here already if he was." She tossed her beer bottle into the river, then said, "Besides, it looks like none of you kids brought fishing rods with you. You got nothing to worry about."

With that, the woman started swinging the garbage bag over her head like a hammer throw in the Olympics. When she let the bag fly, it landed in the brush several yards away. Everybody had a good laugh with her antics and soon settled back to their drinking and general merrymaking.

There were a number of things that concerned the fish warden and me at the moment, not the least of which was the huge bonfire that was burning. There hadn't been any significant rain for months. In fact, the governor of Pennsylvania had issued a statewide burn ban weeks earlier. The littering was disgraceful, but we were more concerned about the fire and the possibility of underage drinking.

As we approached the crowd, we saw a young man and a girl seated in lawn chairs next to each other drinking beer. There was another couple to their right who were also drinking, and four others seated nearby on logs along the bank. The first couple finished their beers and pitched the bottles into the bushes just as we came up from behind.

The woman that the fish warden had cited earlier was first to spot us. "You again!" she shouted. "What do you want this time? I'm not fishing anymore!"

We ignored her outburst and identified ourselves as state conservation officers to the group. Because he hadn't seen all eight of the young people drinking, the fish warden used a field test kit to check the blood alcohol levels of each person. The average age for the girls was between fifteen and sixteen and they all tested over .10%, which made them legally drunk. The males were between seventeen and nineteen and were verified at .02% — relatively "sober." Because none of them were of legal age, we informed all eight that they would be cited for underage drinking which inspired one young man to warn us that his uncle was a police officer and that he would have the tickets fixed by tomorrow morning.

While the fish warden wrote citations for each person, I picked up two dozen beer bottles strewn over a sixty-foot area and started writing additional citations for littering.

Because the two adults who had joined the party were not related to the juveniles and we had no proof that they had supplied the alcohol, they were not charged with anything related to the underage drinking; however, the woman was charged with two incidents of littering, one for the bottle in the river and another for her "hammer throw" into the brush.

When teenagers are cited for underage drinking, law enforcement officers are required to inform their parents. After all of the citations were written and evidence gathered, we doused the bonfire, escorted the teens back to the Tunkhannock launch area, and called their parents to come and get them.

Most of the parents were deeply concerned about the incident and apologized for the trouble their sons and daughters had caused. But the mother of one fifteen-year-old girl who had been intoxicated became angry at us for citing her child. Concerned that her daughter's driver's license might be suspended when she applied for one, she accused us of being cruel, and interested only in our arrest quota for the month. When we reminded her that we'd discovered her daughter and three other girls miles from home in a secluded area with three older males, emphasizing that it was only the girls who were intoxicated, the mother assured us that her daughter could take care of herself. "Who do I call to get this ticket fixed?" She demanded. "I am not going to allow my daughter's license to be suspended."

We informed her that her daughter had the right to a hearing in a court of law and that a judge would decide her fate.

Mom left in a huff with her daughter, shouting, "I'll see you in court!" as she got into her car and drove off.

Hours had passed by now, and it had been difficult enough dealing with the circumstances at hand, but to find a mother so callous toward the health and welfare of her teenage daughter weighed heavily on my mind.

On the way home once again, hoping to finally get some rest, I was sidetracked by a radio call from regional headquarters about a hunter who was lost somewhere on Dutch Mountain. He was last seen going into Tamarack Swamp in a section of wilderness located in State Game Lands 57 known as The Coal Mine (named after an abandoned century old coal mine carved into bedrock). This area is in Forkston Township and extremely remote with extensive forests of hardwoods, black spruce, and other coniferous trees.

Deputy Stover overheard the call from dispatch and messaged me by radio saying that he would meet me at the Coal Mine in thirty minutes. I was relieved to hear this. Marshall was born and raised in Wyoming County and knew that area far better than I did.

I recalled a similar incident years earlier when a woman became lost in the exact same area. It was the first day of bear season and she had gone into the forest to track a bear she had shot. I traveled to the location with Deputy Marshall Stover on that cold and snowy night and stood by while he walked deep into the forest and found her alive and well.

As I traveled toward Forkston, I radioed Wyoming County Communications on the police bandwidth to advise them that we had a lost hunter on the mountain.

"You want fire and rescue up there?" questioned the dispatcher.

"Might be a good idea," I responded. "Someone could be hurt." I couldn't help thinking that someone could even be dead. It's unforgiving country up there laced with vertical rocky overhangs and deep, slippery crevices. I wondered if the individual had been involved in a hunting accident or severely injured in a fall. A thousand possibilities crossed my mind— none of them good.

By the time I reached Forkston, a band of fire and rescue vehicles were heading up Dutch Mountain. They were a welcome sight. We all stopped at the foot of the mountain to put our heads together and formulate a plan. I was to coordinate the procedure and communicate by radio with Mehoopany Fire and Rescue. They were to remain at the top of the mountain by the road while I drove back to the Coal Mine parking lot (a flat surface of bedrock the size of a baseball field near Coalbed Swamp) in my four-wheel-drive patrol vehicle. The two-track going in was very rough and would have been impassible by car or ambulance.

On my way to the Coal Mine, I saw jeep headlights approaching in my rearview mirror. Marshall Stover, I thought. Thank the Lord.

We parked on the rocky flattop by the mine and climbed out of our vehicles. Although it was mid-October, the temperature had dropped into the twenties, so I reached into the back of my Ford Bronco, grabbed a heavy patrol coat and slipped it on to ward off the chill. When I turned around, Marshall Stover was sorting through his gear. He was well prepared with a backpack, compass, two headlamps, flashlights, a sleeping bag, a heavy blanket, assorted food and drinks (including hot coffee), and a first aid kit.

I didn't want him to go into the swamp alone, but my job was to coordinate the rescue, which would have been impossible to do if I went along with him. I handed Marshall my portable radio and wished him well, knowing he'd be able to communicate with me by calling the radio in my patrol car, which gave me a sense of relief.

Marshall no sooner disappeared into the forest when several members of the rescue team arrived in a pickup truck. One of them asked if I wanted Guthrie One on scene (a critical-care helicopter based out of Robert Packard Hospital). I looked up at the cold black sky and watched the moon disappear behind a heavy layer of clouds. Snow began to swirl around us, and the wind suddenly picked up, sending stinging chills through my clothing.

"Yes," I said. "Have them start over here."

Thirty minutes later, I heard the chopper approaching. At first it was a tiny sparkle of lights in the sky, but soon it came so close that the *thump-thump-thump* of its whirling blades seemed to pulsate right through me.

I had radio communications with the pilot, and he informed me that he had spotted a campfire directly below him. The chopper circled the fire several times before casting a one-million-candle-power spotlight down over the fire. The pilot radioed back to me saying that he could see several people standing by the fire dressed in orange clothing. He also said that he could see my deputy heading right for them. "They're just south of him, only a hundred yards away."

The scrub oaks on the mountain were so thick that Deputy Stover could only see a few yards in front of him, but when he spotted the glow of a campfire ahead, he climbed a tree and shined his flashlight toward the people surrounding it, instructing everyone to put out the fire and follow the beam from his flashlight until they reached him.

None of us realized that the people were the lost hunter's family members who had started their own search earlier until Stover radioed the information back to us. They had found the hunter hours ago but became lost themselves on their way out and decided to build a fire hoping to be rescued. Stover shared some food and drinks with the weary travelers, and they soon walked out together as a group.

I had my mic in my hand when the chopper thundered over my Bronco. Guthrie One was about to touch down on the bedrock directly in front of me. As the huge chopper hovered over my head, I could see the silhouette of the surrounding Endless Mountains under the glow of its navigation lights. Snow squalls danced in the landing zone as the whirlybird descended. It was an awesome sight. Here we stood in the middle of a virtual wilderness while this enormous metal beast was descending upon us. For a moment, I felt small and vulnerable, and thought it must be what a field mouse feels like in that final moment when a great horned owl drops down on it. The mere sight of the huge predatory bird putting it into a state of shock.

The chopper landed, its blades idling in a steady *whuff-whuff-whuff* as Deputy Stover walked out of the forest with the lost party. There were five people in total, and they were amazed to see a helicopter standing by. A medic exited the machine, his head held low under the rotating blades as he approached the group. After checking to see if everyone was safe and accounted for, he signaled to the pilot that all was well and hustled back into chopper. We all stood by and stared in awe as the helicopter lifted slowly off the bedrock and disappeared into the night.

As the rescue team transported the lost hunter and his family back to their vehicles, which had been left in the State Game Lands parking lot by the main the road, Marshall Stover and I stayed behind, sitting side by side on a rock ledge as we shared cups of coffee from his thermos. There was a vast blanket of silence now that everyone had left. Soon the clouds parted, bringing a spectacular full moon into view.

"I appreciate what you did out there tonight, Marshall," I said.

He took a sip from his cup and nodded without meeting my eyes. "Glad I could help," he said. "They weren't dressed for a long night in the cold."

I nodded in agreement.

"Nice moon," said Stover.

"Yep."

"Poacher's moon."

"Sure is," I said.

"I've been getting reports of night shooting along Sugar Hollow Road," he said, his tone hinting that he wanted to head over there.

I had no doubt Marshall would be going to Sugar Hollow whether I went with him or not. I wanted to go home, slide into bed, and sleep like a log until morning. Instead, I put my cup to my lips and drained it. "Your coffee is going to keep me up for hours, anyway," I said with an exaggerated sigh. "Might as well make the most of a beautiful night."

Deputy Stover's eyes were wide and bright in the moonlight, and he smiled contentedly.

THE GIFT
PART ONE

There is no benefit in the gifts of a bad man.
~Euripides, *Medea,* 431 BC

A STUNNING OCTOBER SUNRISE had painted the mountains of Wyoming County with a firelike brilliance of reds, yellows, and orange, casting a spell upon me. It was my favorite time of the year, and I couldn't help but gaze out the triple windows in my kitchen at the incredible view as I polished off a plate of bacon, eggs, and toast.

My wife, Maryann, removed a carafe of coffee from the *Mr. Coffee* machine on the counter behind me, poured two cups, and brought them to the table. "Will you be back for lunch?" she asked as she sat across from me and slid a cup my way.

"I don't think so," I said. "I'm heading over to State Game Lands on Dutch Mountain. Archery deer season opens today."

"Dinner then?" she asked.

"For sure," I said with a reassuring smile.

Dutch Mountain was in a remote and mountainous section of my district at the edge of a wild area encompassing several thousand square miles. It took time to drive out there, and once I started patrolling the narrow, rutted two-tracks that snaked through the forests on their way to dozens of hunting camps, I'd be busy most of the day. Still, I didn't anticipate much activity and expected to find most of the camps empty. Bow season didn't attract anywhere near the number of deer hunters as rifle season did, which wouldn't start until November.

Wyoming County is a four-hundred square mile area located in the Endless Mountain region of northeastern Pennsylvania. It's situated on the Allegheny Plateau and bisected by the north branch of the Susquehanna River. The entire county is rural and mountainous with a sprinkling of farms and a population of about twenty-five thousand people. In those days (1990s), the entire county had but one traffic light, which was located in the center of Tunkhannock, the county seat. I had recently transferred there from my initial assignment in Montgomery County and was still learning where all the hunting camps, streams, hollows, and roadways were located in case I ran into trouble and had to call for backup. Dutch Mountain was located in Forkston Township, (one of seventeen townships in the county) a vast forested area with a spider's web of old logging roads and trails that led to secluded hunting camps. It would require many months of exploration before I'd become familiar with the area.

Maryann and I sat for a while and talked about our two children, Jesse, and Sarah, and how they were doing with schoolwork and life in general. Both were asleep upstairs, and it gave us a chance to catch up before I left for the day.

Sarah, our six-year-old, was in first grade. She was sweet, self-confident, energetic, and remarkably athletic for her age, so much so that we had recently signed her up for martial arts classes. Maryann, Jesse, and I had been training in *Tang Soo Do* (also called Korean karate) for some time, and it was nice to have the entire family involved. Jesse was twelve and enjoyed playing baseball and soccer, and participating in swimming competitions. It was a tough age for most boys in seventh grade as they struggled with the peaks and valleys of adolescence, and our son was no exception. Fortunately, schoolwork came easy for him, as his mind worked like a sponge absorbing everything his teachers explained. I secretly wished my own school studies had been so effortless while growing up.

Although my days were busy checking hunters, answering wildlife complaints, stocking pheasants, and dealing with roadkilled deer, I managed to find some time to set traps for beavers, mink and muskrats with a little fox and coyote trapping mixed in when the seasons opened, and would bring Jesse or Sarah along with me whenever possible. Looking back, I think that I enjoyed having the kids with me even more than they did. It gave us time to bond and brought them into a world that few will ever know.

"I'll have dinner ready for six," Maryann said. "I'm making lasagna."

Maryann baked the best homemade meat lasagna on the planet, and I wondered if it was her secret way of making sure I'd be home for dinner tonight. The past week had been hectic with calls about night shooting, and I'd been away almost every evening into the early morning hours.

I picked up my breakfast dishes, took them to the sink, and washed and dried them while Maryann relaxed with her coffee. It was the least I could do. She was a meticulous housekeeper and would keep busy tidying up our home until Jesse and Sarah woke up when she would devote all of her time and attention to them.

"Any plans today?" I asked as I pulled on my boots.

"I'm taking the kids to Riverside Park for lunch," she said beaming. "We're having a picnic!"

I felt guilty not being able to go with them. "That'll be nice," I said. "It's a beautiful day."

The corners of her mouth lifted into a pretty smile. "We'll go to a different park tomorrow after church so you can be there too," she said. "I already have it planned."

I smiled, happy to be included. "I'll see you tonight."

"Love you," she called as I started out the back door.

"Love you too."

I stepped outside into a chilly autumn morning breeze. Cumulus clouds scudded across a deep blue sky like puffy balls of cotton in a frenzied race to some faraway finish line. I filled my lungs with fresh mountain air as the sun peeked above Miller Mountain in the east, glad to be alive.

I kept my state issued green Ford Bronco backed into an offshoot at the side of my driveway, and as I stepped around to the driver's side I momentarily froze. The decapitated and partially skinned carcass of a freshly killed buck deer lay directly alongside my patrol car. It had been caped out with the hide removed from the middle of its ribcage down to the center of its front legs. There was a gaping exit wound in its chest from a high-powered rifle. Judging by the size of the carcass, and the fact that it was caped out, it could have been a trophy buck with an impressive set of antlers. An illegal kill to be sure, as only bow season was open, and I was stunned to see a greeting card pinned to its naked shoulder with a six-inch wooden-handled ice pick.

Snapping on a pair of latex examination gloves, I stooped and carefully removed the ice pick and the card, planning to submit both to the state police crime lab for fingerprints. The card, a Hallmark that could have been purchased anywhere, contained a three-word inscription that sent a chill running down my spine: *THINKING OF YOU.*

State Trooper Gary Wilkes was cruising down Route 29 at the end of his shift just before sunup when he saw the arc of a powerful light sweep across a field several hundred yards ahead. He decked the accelerator and made a hard left on a dirt road where he suspected the spotlight was coming from and soon came upon a Ford pickup truck with Massachusetts tags stopped in the middle of the road.

Wilkes turned on his red emergency lights and pulled behind the truck. The trooper could see two occupants through the rear window as he walked to the driver's door and shined his flashlight into the cab.

Both were males in their mid-thirties and had compound bows, arrows, and a spotlight in the cab with them. The trooper explained that it was illegal to stop along a highway and that spotlighting while in possession of firearms or archery equipment was also unlawful. He was a hunter himself and wasn't concerned about the traffic violation so much as the possibility that the two men planned to jacklight a deer. The road they were on was seldom traveled, which would give them plenty of time to kill a deer and get it back to their vehicle without anyone seeing them.

After checking their identification and transferring the spotlight and archery equipment into the bed of their pickup, he radioed Wyoming County Communications and asked for a game warden to respond.

Deputy Casey Grant happened to be on patrol in the area and overheard the radio communication. He arrived shortly after and secured the suspect's archery equipment and spotlight inside his vehicle for evidence. Since both men were from out of state, Casey knew they would have to be taken before a local district justice to be arraigned before they were released. He also wanted to search the field for a spent arrow or any other signs that a deer had been targeted by the men.

I had just climbed into my Bronco after loading the headless buck onto my big game rack when I heard Casey calling me over the airwaves. I grabbed my mic off the dashboard and thumbed the transmit button, asking what he needed. Casey explained what he had, and I advised him that I was on my way and to stand by until I got there.

Angry and humiliated that someone had brought their grievance to my home, and therefore my family, I fumed as I drove south on Route 29 to meet Deputy Grant. Whoever had left the headless deer on my driveway wanted to make things personal, and that touched a nerve in a way that I'd never experienced before. At the time, I had twenty years on the job with many hundreds of arrests, and no one had ever done anything like this before.

The fact that they had killed a buck out of season, decapitated it, and used the carcass as a sending board for their warped message told me that it was probably someone I had caught poaching deer in the past.

I mulled over the arrests I had made over the past several years. There were a number of deer cases, but only two poachers came to mind as possible contenders: Ned Kolikowsky and Butch Stryker.

I had assisted State Game Warden Chuck Arcovitch with a poaching case that involved Kolikowsky and his partner Delbert Ronson two years earlier. They had been slaughtering deer in Wyoming and Susquehanna Counties almost nightly for months. Many of the deer were left lying in open fields with only their heads removed. Delbert Ronson had been

71

killed in a car crash shortly after we arrested them, but Ned was still around, and I suspected he was still poaching deer.

Ned Kolikowsky was sixteen when he killed his first deer. The fact that he shot it in closed season after sneaking onto his neighbor Sam Browne's property made the experience all the more enjoyable for him. That's just the kind of guy he was.

When Sam Browne heard the shot, he stormed out of the barn in time to see someone dragging a deer from his alfalfa field into the neighboring woods. And although he had suffered crop damage from a burgeoning deer herd all summer long, he hated the fact that someone had come onto his property and shot one right under his nose, so he walked back into the barn, picked up his wall phone, and called the Pennsylvania Game Commission.

State Game Warden Chuck Arcovitch picked up Kolikowsky's trail by following blood spatters and occasional boot scuffs through the woods. When he finally broke through the trees, he came upon a two-story house that stood alone on a small plot of ground. Fresh footprints led through the damp morning grass directly to the house, but there was no sign of a deer being dragged through the grass.

Chuck went directly to the house and knocked on the front door. It opened immediately, with Ned Kolikowsky's huge frame filling the doorway. He seemed immense for his youthful age, standing six-foot-three and a good two-hundred-twenty pounds.

"Saw ya coming across the field," he said with a crooked smile. "Looking for somebody?"

Chuck asked if his parents were home, hesitant to interview a juvenile without an adult present.

Kolikowsky told him that his mother was sleeping upstairs and asked him to come back later.

Returning later was not an option. Chuck had no choice but to push on. "Somebody killed a deer on Sam Browne's property," he said. "I tracked him here."

Ned denied knowing anything about the deer. He stepped back and put a finger to his lips. "*Shhh!*" he said cocking his head toward the second floor. "Come in and look for yourself. Just please be quiet."

Chuck went through the house looking for deer hairs or drops of blood but found nothing indicating that a deer had been brought inside.

About a year later, Chuck ran into Kolikowsky again. After a little small talk, Chuck asked the million-dollar question: "Ned, where did you hide the deer that day I searched your house?"

Ned Kolikowsky grinned mischievously. "Upstairs in my bedroom," he said. "Under my mattress."

It was several years later that Chuck Arcovitch and I searched a rundown farmhouse where Ned Kolikowsky and Delbert Ronson lived after getting a tip that they had been killing and decapitating antlered deer almost nightly in our districts.

When we finished searching the property, by all counts, it amounted to the largest accumulation of unlawfully killed game seized in a single operation during our combined careers. Charges against the men totaled more than twenty thousand dollars, and I'd heard rumblings that Kolikowsky wanted to exact revenge on Chuck and me for the huge fines he received. Judging from his past behavior, coupled with his reckless personality, I put him right behind Butch Stryker as a prime suspect for the headless deer in my driveway.

Stryker was a career poacher who I'd had a number of run-ins with over the years. It all started shortly after I transferred into Wyoming County and had only intensified from there. But that first encounter was the worst by far, and Stryker seemed to harbor a deep-seated hatred for me ever since.

What had started out as a simple untagged deer violation quickly escalated into a full-scale brawl between Stryker's family and me. Stryker made the mistake of coming at me after being warned to stay back. I hit him hard, knocking him to the ground, but he quickly jumped up and came at me again. His brother and his wife both grabbed him from behind and pulled him back just as he threw a roundhouse punch that glanced off my jaw. As a result, he ended up in jail with the felony charge of assaulting a police officer added to his lengthy arrest record. Stryker had hurled a number of veiled threats at me over the years, and I always believed that one day he would follow through on one of them.

Deputy Casey Grant was standing by the open tailgate of a blue Ford pickup when I pulled behind his patrol car and parked. Two men stood beside him, both in their thirties and dressed in camo hunting gear. He motioned for the men to stay where they were and walked over to meet me as I climbed out of my Bronco.

"They admit that they were spotlighting deer," he said. "But they look nervous to me, and I think they might have taken a shot at one. Might've hit it, too. We need to check the field alongside their truck. That's where they were spotlighting when Trooper Wilkes came by."

"Massachusetts, huh," I said, glancing over his shoulder at the tags on the truck. "Long way from home."

"That's what I'm thinking. And when you come this far, you don't want to go home empty-handed. I have a strong feeling that we'll find something in that field once we get in there."

"Why don't you go take a look while I get acquainted with our suspects," I said.

Casey reached into his back pocket and pulled out a notepad and handed it to me. "That has all their information on it: names, addresses, home phone numbers, hunting license numbers—everything you need for their citations."

I stuffed the notebook into my jacket pocket and thanked him. Although he'd only been with me for one year, he learned fast and was a hard worker, spending most of his free time on patrol during the various hunting seasons which ran from early September through January.

While Casey searched the weedy five-acre field for evidence that might link our suspects to some kind of hunting activity, I stood at the back of their truck and asked them a few softball questions, hoping to find out more about them and what brought them to Wyoming County from distant Massachusetts.

Their names were Sal and Guido. Longtime friends and hunting companions who had come back to Pennsylvania for a few days to hunt, they told me. Both men had been from nearby Scranton until moving to Massachusetts a number of years ago to work in construction.

"So, you both like it here," I said. "I do too. It's beautiful country and most deer hunters bypass the entire county, driving straight through on their way to Bradford and Tioga Counties where more deer are killed. I'm surprised you didn't do the same thing."

Sal said, "More deer are killed in those counties because more hunters are moving them. It's just as good here if you know where to look." He paused to stare into the field where Casey was scouting for sign, then said, "When we lived in Scranton, we always came here to hunt. But there's nothing going on in Scranton anymore, so we left. They're building everywhere in Massachusetts."

I looked at Guido. He stood fencepost straight, head bowed, his eyes refusing to meet mine. He was visibly shaken, and I wanted to take advantage of it.

"Is that right, Guido?" I asked.

"Huh?" he mumbled, glancing up at me briefly before examining his boots again.

I stepped closer. "Sal says they're building everywhere in Massachusetts, is that right?"

Guido shrugged. "I guess so."

"I understand that someone was shining a spotlight in the field just before the trooper arrived. Is that right, too, Guido?"

He nodded without looking up at me.

"Did one of you shoot at a deer, Guido?" I asked. "Is that what you two were searching for when the trooper came by— a deer that ran off after being hit it with an arrow?"

Guido raised his head slowly and looked at me with frightened eyes. And for a moment, I thought he was about to talk. But he glanced over at Sal and quickly bowed his head again.

A whistle came from the field. I turned to see Casey standing a hundred yards away waving his arm at me. I waved back and he gave me a thumbs up. He had found something: a dead deer, blood, an arrow? At the moment I couldn't know, but I felt certain that whatever it was would bolster our case against the two men.

Casey marched back from the field with purpose in his step, and I knew that Sal and Guido saw it too. As he drew near, I could see he was holding an arrow in his right hand.

"I found a dead eight-pointer back there," he said, when he reached us. He held the arrow across both palms so we could all get a good look at it. It was a 100-grain Grizzly aluminum broadhead. "A heart shot," he added, looking over at me. "Same arrow as the ones they brought with them. I have them in my truck if you want to take a look. Perfect match."

Sal's jaw was set tight as a clam.

Guido looked like he was about to cry.

"Anything you want to say about this?" I asked them.

Guido let out a withering sigh and looked over at Sal. "I can't do this anymore, Sal" he said, his voice breaking. "Sorry, but they got us cold."

"Shut up, Guido!" Sal snapped at him. "Don't say anything more."

I took a step toward Sal. "You need to calm down," I said. "I'm talking to Guido, not you. One more outburst like that and I'll charge you with interference along with the deer you killed."

Sal glowered at me.

I turned to Guido. "You were saying…?"

Guido side-stepped away from Sal. Then said, "I was driving and Sal was standing in the bed of the truck with his bow when we saw the buck. It was close to the road. Couldn't miss it. I stopped, shut off the engine, and slid over to the passenger side with my spotlight and lit it up. The buck ran twenty yards and stopped. Then it turned broadside to us and Sal shot at it. It sounded like a good hit when the deer ran off, so I started shining the field to see how far it got when we saw headlights coming. Sal jumped out of the truck and got behind the steering wheel real quick. The next thing we knew, the cop had his red lights on us, and, well, here we are, caught cold."

I told them that they were both facing six-hundred-dollar fines and that we would have to escort them to the local district justice's office for an immediate hearing, explaining that they would have to post financial security for the entire amount before they could leave the state.

"You gotta be kidding me," whined Sal. "We don't have that kind of money with us."

"That's the law," I said. "You're both under arrest right now. I want you to get back in your truck and follow me to the judge's office. My deputy's truck will be right behind you, so don't try to wonder off."

Judge O'Rourke walked into his courtroom dressed in a black robe clearly annoyed. He was in his fifties, but his thick white hair and brushy eyebrows made him look older. He looked us over with black, hawkish eyes, his face set in a deep scowl. There were three district judges in Wyoming County, and it was his turn to be on call for the weekend. Judge O'Rourke was not friendly toward game wardens, or any other police officer for that matter, and I had no idea what I might be in for. Familiar with his background, I was afraid he'd be more inclined to blame me instead of the two poachers I'd brought before him for dragging him out of bed that morning.

He sat at his bench (a large wooden desk at the front of the courtroom), raised his gavel to his shoulder and brought it crashing down on the desktop. "Court is now in session!" he barked. "Make it quick!"

Sal and Guido sunk down in their chairs. I didn't blame them. They were far from home, in front of a grumpy judge, and didn't have enough money on hand to pay their fines.

Fortunately, my case was solid and uncomplicated. I didn't expect to keep the judge long. I had an illegally killed deer shot with an arrow that matched the arrows found in the defendants' vehicle, and I had an admission of guilt from Guido. The men knew it was game over, so when Judge O'Rourke read my citations out loud and asked them how they would plea. Both men pleaded guilty.

Because Sal and Guido lived out of state, Judge O'Rourke told them they had two choices: pay their fines or go directly to jail.

Guido sprang from his chair, eyes wild with panic. "But judge, we don't have that much money with us. Please, Your Honor, allow me to call home and I'll make arrangements to have the money sent here today."

The judge stared at Guido over the rim of his glasses, his jaw clenched in irritation. "You have one phone call," he cautioned. "That's all you're getting. Make it count."

Guido sighed in relief. "Thank you, Your Honor."

"Follow me," replied the judge, rising briskly from the bench. "There's a phone in the other room."

While Casey remained with Sal, I accompanied Guido and the judge out of the courtroom through a side entryway that led to the front office. There were two desks in the center of the room, both stacked with court papers, manila folders, and other assorted documents. Had it been a weekday, two female clerks would have been seated at their desks organizing files, preparing documents, and scheduling appointments.

"Make your call," the judge said, pointing to a phone on an adjacent desk. I watched as Guido lifted the handset off a black desk phone, put it to his ear, and started pushing buttons with his index finger. There was a hush in the room as we waited to see if anyone answered, so quiet that I could hear the low hum of his ringtone on the other end of the line. It rang three times. There was an audible *click*, then a woman's voice: "Hello?"

"Maria!" Guido said frantically. "I'm in trouble."

"What happened?" she asked, alarm in her voice.

"Me and Sal got arrested by the game warden. We're in Pennsylvania. I need you to contact my lawyer, Marcello, right now and have him call the phone number I'm about to give you." He looked over at the judge, eyes pleading. The judge shook his head wearily and nodded that it was okay.

Fortunately for Sal and Guido, the attorney returned a call within a matter of minutes and spoke directly to Judge O'Rourke. He identified himself, gave his license number from the American Bar Association, and made arrangements to wire the necessary funds to pay both fines. Sal and Guido were on their way home shortly thereafter.

"Where did the headless deer come from?" asked Casey when we stepped out the front door of Judge O'Rourke's office into the parking lot. Our vehicles were parked parallel to each other near the building.

"Somebody left it in my driveway this morning," I said, as we walked over to the carcass tied down on my big game rack at the back of my Bronco. It was a massive buck, so large that both ends of the deer draped over the rack's frame almost touching the ground. I briefed Casey about the note and the ice pick.

"Any idea who it was?"

"Two people come to mind, but it's just a guess."

"Anybody I know?"

"No, it was before you came on."

"Ice pick, huh," remarked Casey, shaking his head. "That's pretty sick."

"Yeah," I said. "Pretty sick. I'm just glad I saw it before Maryann or the kids did."

Casey nodded in agreement.

I said, "I want you to patrol the northern end of the county. I'll head south, there's somebody I want to see around noon."

"One of your suspects?"

"Yep."

T en large turkey vultures lifted off and perched in nearby branches like grim gargoyles overlooking the grounds of an ancient castle as I backed my Bronco along a two-track and stopped at the deer pit. Some of the birds had been so gorged with rotting meat that they expelled projectile-vomit to lose weight and escape from the six-foot-deep trench that had been carved into the earth by a backhoe.

I shouldered open the door, slid out, and walked to the edge of the pit. The remains of a dozen deer lay scattered at the bottom. Some reduced to skeletons over time, others in various stages of decomposition. All were roadkills that I had dumped on different days earlier in the month. The stench of rotting deer permeated the air, a foul smell that I would never get used to no matter how many visits I made to the pit, and there had been hundreds over the years.

At least it wouldn't go to a complete waste I thought as I unhooked three rubber bungie cords securing the headless buck to my big game rack and dragged the carcass to the edge of the pit. One good shove with my boot and it rolled to the bottom in an ungraceful heap for the vultures to pick at.

Unlike most birds, airborne turkey vultures have an acute sense of smell that can catch the scent of dead animals below the forest canopy. Their stomach acid is extremely acidic so they can digest almost anything, including carcasses tainted with anthrax, tuberculosis, and rabies without getting sick. Although vultures were the primary visitors at the pit, I could also see bear and coyote droppings nearby.

The only part of the job that I really hated was picking up roadkilled deer. My record was nine in one day, but I knew of other game wardens that had retrieved many more in a single day. With approximately fifty thousand deer killed on the highways in Pennsylvania each year, removing the carcasses could be a daunting task for game wardens in districts with a high volume of traffic.

Fortunately, Wyoming County was not in the same category as Montgomery and Philadelphia counties where I had been assigned for thirteen years before transferring north. While stationed there, I averaged two or three roadkilled deer every week. But there were times when I'd spend an entire day dragging rotting deer carcasses writhing with maggots off the highways. It didn't do much good for my image (or the Game Commission's for that matter) to have the carcasses exposed on my deer rack, some with multiple broken legs dangling off the edge, as I drove through the congested highways of my metropolitan district in a marked patrol car.

With the headless buck disposed of, I climbed back into my Bronco and began to patrol the surrounding state game lands. There was over a hundred thousand acres of wilderness to explore in this particular tract, and I didn't expect to see a large volume of bow hunters anywhere. My best bet would be to visit several of the interior parking lots the Game Commission had built over the years. With any luck, I'd come across a few hunters as they exited the woods with their kills heading back to their vehicles.

Along the way, I came across a Chevrolet sedan that had pulled off and parked alongside the road. There was an orange-clad hunter in a portable treestand a short distance into the woods. He looked thin, maybe 120 pounds, and stood less than five feet tall. On the small side for a grown man, I thought. Because young hunters must be accompanied by an adult or someone eighteen or older, depending on their age, I grabbed my field glasses off the passenger seat for a quick look. Dialing in the lens, I focused on the hunter's face. He was looking right at me. Definitely a boy well under the age of eighteen.

I pulled off the road, parked behind the Chevrolet, and exited my Bronco in full uniform. As I walked toward the boy, he placed his bow flat on the bottom of the treestand, keeping his eyes on me the entire time.

"State game warden," I said, standing directly below him. "How old are you?"

81

"Fourteen," he responded. He wore an orange vest and ballcap along with blue Levi jeans and black hunting boots.

"Climb down and bring your hunting equipment with you," I said.

I watched as he lowered his bow and field quiver to the ground on a thin nylon rope before descending a metal ladder. When he reached the ground, I took his hunting license from the plastic holder attached to the back of his hunting vest and looked it over. His name was James Ring. He looked older than his age and could have passed for sixteen.

"Are you with anyone?" I asked.

"Yes, my father. You parked behind his car."

"Where is he?"

"In his treestand."

I scanned the open woods, looking in every direction, but couldn't see any sign of another hunter. "Call your father," I said. "Ask him to come over here."

James cupped a hand to the side of his mouth and hollered for his father. In the distance I heard a faint shout-back. James called out again and after a minute or so, I saw a camouflaged hunter wearing an orange ballcap break over a rise a hundred yards away and come hustling toward us.

"What's going on here?" he asked as he approached, somewhat out of breath. He was of medium height and thickset with broad shoulders. He had the stern face of someone always in command.

"Your son is too young to be hunting alone," I said.

He stepped toward me, practically in my face. It was too close. I took one step back.

"What do you mean he was hunting alone?" he asked, his tone brisk and demanding. "Didn't you just hear him calling me? You saw me coming. I was here in minutes!"

At the time, I had no intention of fining anyone and simply wanted the boy to be safe. I also knew it was embarrassing for a father to be confronted by a law enforcement officer in front of his son, and believed that was the reason for his apparent anger.

"The law requires you to be physically alongside your son at all times," I said. "Close enough to see what he's doing so you can correct him if necessary. That would have been impossible in your case."

"Look, warden, you're being ridiculous," he said. "My son took a hunter education class and passed it with aces. Besides, I taught him everything he needed to know. He's very mature for his age and doesn't need me or anyone else babysitting him like some nine-year-old."

I was losing patience with the man, and I felt embarrassed for the boy. His father was setting a poor example by arguing with a law enforcement officer in front of his son, especially when the law was black and white. The boy needed to be with an adult. Period. I didn't have the power to allow James to hunt alone, even if he was "very mature for is age" as his father claimed. Nor could I walk away, thereby allowing James to climb back into his treestand with his bow once I drove off. Considering his father's attitude, I was certain that's what would happen if I turned and left them.

"I want to see your hunting license," I told him.

"You want to see *my* hunting license!" he snorted. "What for?"

"Turn around," I said flatly. Like all hunters in Pennsylvania at the time, his hunting license was in a plastic holder pinned to the clothing on the center of his back.

He glared at me with hatred in his eyes, his cheeks turning blood red. "This is outright harassment!" he bellowed. "You walked in here like you own the place and ruined our hunt. You're not even a cop, just some minor-league civil servant who thinks he's a big shot. Somebody needs to put you in your place, pal!"

He looked like he was about to explode, and for a moment, I thought he might physically attack me. I stepped back with my right foot, preparing to defend myself if he made his move.

"Dad!" his son shouted. "Why are you doing this?"

Ring whipped his head around and looked at his son, then back to me. I watched as he uncurled his fists and his temper began to recede.

"You were right about your son," I said. "He is mature for his age."

He nodded in silence.

"You need to turn around so I can check your license," I said.

He studied me for a moment, as if deciding whether or not to comply. Then he shook his head with indignation and whirled around in a huff.

I removed his cardboard hunting license from its clear plastic holder and flipped it open. His name was David Ring, age forty-three. He lived in neighboring Luzerne County. His deer tags were attached and everything was in order.

I stuffed the license into my inside jacket pocket and started walking away.

"Where are you going with my license?" asked Ring, bewildered by my move.

"Over to my vehicle."

"What for?"

"That's where I keep my citations," I said over my shoulder.

David Ring followed several yards behind me, yammering away about how stupid the law was as I walked through the woods to my Bronco and opened the driver's side door and slid inside. Seated comfortably, I closed the door and retrieved an aluminum citation clipboard from the console between the front seats and pulled a citation out from the hinged storage compartment and clipped it to the writing plate. Ring stood outside my door staring angrily at me through the window as I pulled a pen from my shirt pocket and began writing. When I finished, I carefully detached his copy from the perforated multiple-layered document, exited my vehicle, and stood in front of him.

"Yours," I said, handing him the citation along with his hunting license. It was a fifty dollar fine.

Ring snatched them from my fingers, his lips curling into a snarl as he looked over the citation. "I'm gonna fight this," he said bitterly. "This ain't right."

"Your choice," I said. "The judge's address is on the citation along with instructions on how to proceed."

"Thanks for ruining my son's day," he grunted. "Hope you enjoyed yourself."

Eager to be shed of the man, I slid back into my patrol car, started the engine, and backed onto the roadway. Ring stood at the edge of the woods and watched; a nasty scowl pasted on his face as I drove away.

It was getting close to noon, so I started working my way back toward town, hoping to find Butch Stryker. I knew where he hung out most afternoons, and wanted to get back into town. Along the way, it suddenly occurred to me that Ned Kolikowsky had been on probation for a burglary charge when Arcovitch and I arrested him for deer poaching. I stopped at a general store on Route 6 and used the phone booth outside to make a call. After feeding two quarters into the slot at the top of the payphone, I waited for a dial tone then started pushing buttons for a call to the Susquehanna County Probation Office.

A female clerk answered and I identified myself and asked to speak with Kolikowsky's probation officer.

"You mean *Ned* Kolikowsky?" she asked, emphasizing his first name.

"Yes."

"He's not on probation anymore," she said, "but I'll connect you to Ronnie Platt; he was the last officer to deal with him."

I waited on hold while disco music played in the background. After a moment, Platt picked up. "Wasserman," he said, his voice deep and authoritative. "I remember your name. We assisted you and Arcovitch with a search warrant for Ned Kolikowsky and Delbert Ronson about two years ago."

"That's right," I said. "I'd like to talk to Ned. I was hoping you could give me an address."

"No can do," he said. "Kolikowsky moved out of the state a few months ago after his probation ended. We lost contact with him. His buddy, Delbert Ronson, is dead by the way. Hope you're not looking for him too."

"No, just Ned. But not anymore if he left the state."

"Sorry I couldn't be more helpful," said Platt.

I hung up, all the more determined to find Butch Stryker and settle things between us.

I was minutes away from town when a dispatcher contacted me by radio to report that a woman named Geena Caine just called about a red fox pestering her German shepherd. "It's there right now," he said. "And it's pacing between her house and the dog's pen."

"Ten four," I said into my mic. "Give me an address."

My meeting with Stryker would have to wait. When a fox noses around a dog's pen in the middle of the day, it's most likely due to rabies or distemper. We already had two foxes and several raccoons test positive for rabies during the past several months, all shot by local farmers. My fear was that the animal was most likely rabid, so I started for Geena Caine's house hoping to arrive before the fox disappeared.

The property was a good distance away, and although I drove as fast as I could, it was still a half-hour before I pulled into her driveway and parked. Geena Caine was in her early thirties, attractive, and slim. She was standing on her front porch waiting for me wearing a green cotton blouse, dark blue jeans, and brown cowboy boots. Her blonde hair was combed back into a ponytail that fell below her shoulders.

"It went into the woods," she cried as I opened the door of my patrol car and started to get out. "It was here a little while ago, then it ran away and I haven't seen it since."

Hoping to get a shot at the fox, I grabbed a .22 Marlin rifle from the gunrack attached to the back of my passenger seat and walked into the wooded area behind her house. Brittle leaves crunched under my boots as I searched for the fox, and so when Geena's dog started barking, I thought it was due to the sound of my footfalls until I heard her cry out.

"It's back!" she called. "Hurry! It's trying to get at my dog."

I ran out of the woods just in time to see the fox lunge at the dog's pen as if it wanted to break through the wire mesh and tear it apart. Meanwhile, the much larger German shepherd stood nose-to-nose with the fox, barking furiously as globs of saliva flew from its mouth.

I was too far away to shoot at the fox without risking harm to the dog, and when I started to move in for a better shot it scampered off to the back of the house. I chased after the fox, reaching the other side of the house just in time to see it heading into the woods again. Hoping to get a clear shot, I followed after the fox on foot but soon lost sight of it.

Thinking it might pay the German shepherd another visit, I went back to the house and stood by the dog's pen waiting to see if it would return. The shepherd must have thought the same thing, for it stood statue-like in its cage, sniffing at the wind to catch scent of the fox while paying me no mind.

When a window directly behind me suddenly squeaked open, I wheeled around to see Geena Caine's face staring at me from the other side.

"Is it gone?" she whispered anxiously.

"It ran into the woods," I said. "I'm going to wait here for a while."

Her eyes dropped to the rifle in my hands. "Do you have to shoot it?" she asked, her eyes meeting mine. "Can't you catch it and take it somewhere?"

"Sorry," I said. "It has to be put down. Foxes don't act like this unless they're sick. They're afraid of dogs and they don't hang around peoples' homes in broad daylight. Judging by the way this one is acting, I believe it has rabies."

"Rabies!" she breathed. "Oh no! What about Jasper?"

The German shepherd turned its head and looked up at her at the sound of his name. I noticed that Jasper didn't have a collar; therefore, no visible rabies tag.

"Has he had rabies shots?" I asked.

She bit her lower lip and shook her head.

"You need to do that," I told her.

"Do you think Jasper will get rabies?"

"There was no physical contact with the fox," I said. "He should be fine, but you should get him to a vet later today or tomorrow to be safe."

"I will," she promised. Then: "How long will you stay here?"

I checked my wristwatch; it was almost noon. Butch Stryker was on my mind.

Rabies, I knew, was a deadly disease caused by a virus that attacks the nervous system. The virus is secreted in saliva and is usually transmitted to people and animals by a bite from an infected animal. Rabies can also be transmitted when saliva from a rabid animal comes in contact with an open cut on the skin or comes in contact with the eyes, nose, or mouth of a person or animal. Once the outward signs of the disease emerge, rabies is nearly always fatal. In fact, I was aware of only one case in the world where a human was infected with rabies and managed to survive.

Once the rabies virus enters the body, it travels along the nerves to the brain. Wild animals with rabies usually display a range of telling signs, including aggression, staggering, immobility, and, when close to death, convulsions. Aggressive behavior is common, but rabid wild animals often lose their fear of humans, and will walk right up to people. Wild animals with rabies that are usually only seen at night may be out wandering about in the daytime, as the red fox on Geena Caine's property was doing.

The saving grace with rabies is the vaccine, which is readily available for humans (and most domestic animals). The catch is that you must get the shots before the virus incubates in your body. The vaccinations are given as a series of injections over a two-week period, and will save your life. But rabies aside, animal bites can be extremely painful and can cause a host of serious problems including bacterial infections, broken teeth embedded in the wound, and the possibility of nerve and blood vessel damage. With those thoughts in mind, I was about to go look for the fox again when Jasper started barking as the fox broke out of the woods fifty yards away. It was making a beeline for Jasper's cage, so I shouldered my rifle and waited for a good body shot.

Because the brain of an animal presumed to have rabies must be submitted to a state lab for examination by a microbiologist, a head shot was out of the question due to the possibility of missing parts of the brain, which would cause the sample to be unacceptable for examination.

When the fox was twenty feet away, Jasper lunged at it inside his pen and barked furiously, causing the fox to sit on its haunches with its head cocked and stare curiously at the dog. It offered a perfect opportunity for a clean shot, so I took aim and sent a .22 long rifle hollow point into its heart, killing the poor creature almost instantly.

Geena Caine heard the rifle shot from inside her house and looked out the open window by Jasper's pen to see me standing over the fox.

"Is that the same fox that came after Jasper?" she called out.

I told her it was, and asked if she had a large cardboard box that I could put the carcass into along with a bottle of Clorox.

Geena said she did, and after a minute she carried a grocery storage box out to me along with the Clorox. After putting the carcass inside the box with gloved hands, I doused the area where it had lain with bleach to make sure any blood or saliva would be neutralized. The next step was to remove the head and package it in a small container (which I didn't have, nor did Geena) so it could be shipped to the department of health. The body would have to be disposed of as well, which meant a trip all the way back to the deer pit in Forkston.

The Pennsylvania Department of Agriculture had a branch office in Tunkhannock. Hoping I could save time by getting someone there to help me, I drove directly over, parked my patrol car by the building, and carried the boxed critter inside.

Gladys McPherson, a middle-aged woman with auburn hair, wire rimmed glasses, and sparkling blue eyes was sitting at the front desk, her fingers dancing across the computer keyboard at lightning speed as I walked in. She looked up at me and smiled.

"Hello, Bill," she said, rising from her desk. "What do you have for us this time?"

"A red fox," I said.

She cocked an eyebrow. "Judging by the size of the box, you have more than just its head in there."

I nodded that she was right, then told her about Geena Caine and her dog, Jasper. "I was hoping Phil would do the dirty work for me," I said. "I have someplace I need to be."

She took a blank sheet of paper and a pen from her desk and handed it to me, a sly twinkle in her eye. "Write down Geena Caine's address so we can notify her if it comes back positive for rabies. Then shoo before Phil comes back from lunch. If you're not here, he can't very well refuse, now can he?"

Butch Stryker's black Harley Davidson motorcycle stood in the center of the only handicap space in the entire parking lot of the Beer and Brisket Tavern as I pulled in and parked next to it. Hanging from the handlebar was a blue and white disability parking placard issued by the state of Pennsylvania. I couldn't help but wonder how he got it, or even if it belonged to him.

I'd had a number of run-ins with Stryker over the years, and he always seemed to be in good physical condition. He could operate an ATV like nobody else, and he easily outran me only two years ago when he spotted me questioning his hunting buddy, Elmer Crowe.

Crowe had just killed an illegal doe in a wooded area when I confronted him about it. While questioning him, I spotted a red-haired figure in camouflage clothing watching us from afar. Certain it was Stryker, I quickly moved toward him, but six-foot-four Butch Stryker with his long legs and considerable head start ran like the wind and soon escaped on an ATV hidden in the woods. When I found Stryker in a treestand later that week and called him down, he descended the wooden cross boards nailed to the trunk with ease, and didn't even bother footing the last three rungs. Instead, he leaped from the tree, spinning 180 degrees in the air so he'd face me when his boots hit the ground. Although he'd plummeted six feet, he landed with the buoyant agility of a jungle cat. Then, smiling cockily, he strode toward me with his head in the air.

Although I was surprised by the handicap placard, it was no surprise to see his Harley parked at the Beer and Brisket. The tavern was on a main highway that I often traveled to get home, and I'd seen it there many times around noon and on some evenings late into the night. His time was his own and he kept odd hours. Stryker was self-employed doing excavation work wherever he could find jobs, which wasn't all that often in rural Wyoming County.

There were a dozen vehicles in the parking lot of the tavern. Most were aging four-wheel-drive pickups belonging to local hunters. Some had gunracks in full display hanging behind their rear windows, others were festooned with bumper stickers and assorted decals pledging allegiance to the NRA and various hunting fraternities.

I was in full uniform when I pushed through the front door and walked into the tavern. It had the atmosphere of a western saloon, with large, framed paintings of Custer's Last Stand, Teddy Roosevelt with his Rough Riders, and other similar works of art hanging on wood-paneled walls along with the mounted heads of white-tailed deer, black bears, and an assortment of trophy game fish. Twenty round tables filled the room, most with hunters and other local folks seated for lunch. Some stared as I walked past, others looked down at their plates, pretending not to see me. I wondered what they might have hidden back at their hunting camps.

The bar was at the far end of the tavern with ten stools lined up in front of it. Butch Stryker sat alone at the center of the bar with his back toward me, his giveaway red hair tied in a long ponytail. A towering six-foot-wide mirror hung on the wall directly behind the bar, flanked on both sides by bottles of whiskey, bourbon, and rye. A stout bartender with a gunfighter's mustache was cleaning glasses at a sink behind the bar when he looked at Stryker and chinned toward me. Stryker raised his head and stared at me through the mirror with hooded eyes as I approached, his expression blank.

I pulled out a bar stool, leaving one empty between us, and sat while meeting his gaze in the mirror.

Stryker rolled his eyes and snorted. "Don't tell me you're gonna sit there and ruin my lunch," he said into the mirror.

I turned in my stool and faced him. "I came to talk to you about the deer."

He was in his late thirties with the flushed complexion of a working alcoholic. He was dressed in a camouflage jacket hooded in the back and brown canvas field pants with black steel-toe work boots. There was a half-full glass of beer and a shot of whiskey on the table in front of him. Stryker put the shot glass to his lips, tossed his head back, and drained it. He set the glass on the counter and gestured for the bartender to bring another, then he turned toward me, his face pinched into a scowl of contempt. "Deer? I don't know what you're talking about, game warden."

The bartender set a fresh shot of whiskey in front of Stryker and took the empty. He looked over at me. "What'll it be, chief?"

"Nothing right now."

"Suit yourself," he said. "How about you, Butch? We have the Burly Brisket on special today."

Stryker took a swallow of his beer, set the glass down and shook his head. "Maybe later, Roscoe. Not right now."

Roscoe looked at me with a frown of disapproval. Then he turned to serve two men who had just sat down at the end of the bar.

Stryker watched Roscoe walk off, then he turned back to me. "Why are you here, Wasserman? I'm not hunting, so I got no business with you."

"Somebody left a deer with its head cut off in my driveway," I said. "I found it this morning."

Stryker grinned mockingly. "So...?"

"There was a greeting card pinned to the carcass with an icepick," I said.

"An early Christmas present for the game warden," he mused. And a card too. How thoughtful."

He downed another shot of whiskey and set the glass down with a hard rap to attract the bartender. "And the fact that you're here, telling me about it, must mean you think *I* did it."

"Stay off my property," I said. "Leave my family out of this or you'll regret it."

Stryker's expression hardened. "You don't scare me, Wasserman," he grunted. "The only thing I'm gonna regret is that I didn't think of it myself."

I eased myself off the bar stool, pulled out my wallet, and put two dollars on the counter for the bartender.

"Remember what I said," I told him as I walked away.

THE GIFT

PART TWO

Cry "Havoc!" and let slip the dogs of war.
~Shakespeare, *Julius Caesar*

EARL WALTON DIDN'T LIKE ALCOHOL. Growing up with alcoholic parents, he had witnessed firsthand the devastating effect it could have on people. His folks fought every night for no other reason than that they were drunk, their senseless bickering sometimes descending into physical abuse. He'd lost count of the times his mother had her ribs broken or went to work with makeup covering a fresh black eye. Earl's father had acquired his share of bruises over the years, too. One time his mother wacked him over the head with an iron skillet so hard it almost killed him. He was in the hospital for two weeks. Earl's folks stopped drinking after that. At least for a little while. But gradually they started again. And with the drinking came the fighting. And with the fighting came the abuse, both verbal and physical. So, when Earl turned eighteen he left home, secretly hoping his parents would come after him, beg him to stay, promise him they'd quit drinking. Tell him they loved him.

But they didn't come.

And he never saw them again.

Inside, the dimly lit bar was packed to the rafters. Earl knew it would be. The November deer season always brought crowds of hunters into the place on Saturday nights. Most were seated in small groups at round wooden tables as they played poker and swapped lies over bottles of beer and shots of whiskey. The barflies, as Earl thought of them, were loud with their boasting of the day's hunt; their drunken howls and boisterous guffaws almost drowning out the jukebox as it boomed with Kenny Rogers singing *The Gambler*.

Earl Walton strolled through a thick haze of cigarette smoke with the easy rolling gait of a barroom brawler, his entire being exuding self-confidence. He was twenty-three but looked thirty. Short and thickset with a broad forehead and a neck as wide as his jaw, he had brown hair cut military short, deep chestnut eyes, and ears permanently deformed and swollen. A former state champion wrestler in high school, his cauliflower ears were the result of extensive mat time grappling with opponents. Some of the patrons glanced up at him as he passed, then quickly looked away when he met their eyes.

Dimitri, a fiftyish, brutish-looking bartender nearly seven feet tall, kept one eye on Earl as he wiped down the counter with a damp cloth. There were fifteen stools lined up at the bar. All were taken. Dimitri knew Earl could be trouble, and hoped he'd behave himself. They had business to tend to, and he didn't want any problems.

Earl walked to the center of the bar and shoved his ample weight between two men in their mid-thirties seated side by side while having a conversation. He looked straight ahead as he leaned into the bar and slowly spread his elbows across the smooth granite countertop, sliding their mugs of beer aside.

The men exchanged looks of utter astonishment.

"Hey! What do you think you're doing?" grunted the man on his right. He was much taller than Earl with a rangy cowboy build.

Earl ignored him. "The usual," he said to Dimitri (the usual for Earl meant a whiskey glass filled with Diet Coke).

Cowboy looked at Dimitri and shook his head with disgust. He couldn't believe what just happened. The bartender waggled a finger, signaling him not to make a move. But Cowboy couldn't let it go. He slid off his stool, stepped behind Earl, and began jackhammering a stiff finger into his shoulder. "Hey! I'm talking to you, jerk!" he shouted.

In one swift move, Earl Walton spun around and brought a cocked elbow crashing into Cowboy's jaw, sending him reeling backwards into a table where four men were playing poker. Game cards, dollar bills, and bottles of beer flew in all directions as the table pitched and then crashed to the floor with Cowboy sprawled over it.

Cowboy's partner hopped off his stool and rushed to his side as the four poker players grabbed at the cash scattered across the hardwood floor.

Everyone in the bar stopped and stared as Cowboy staggered to his feet with the help of his friend. Blood trickled down the side of his mouth, his eyes bulged in their sockets. It was all he could do to remain standing as Earl strode toward him with his heavy hands balled into tight fists.

Dimitri had seen enough. He jerked the wall plug from its socket behind the jukebox cutting off Kenny Rogers in midverse: *You've got to know when to hold 'em, know when to fold 'em—rrrrrrrrip!*

"Stop it right now!" Dimitri roared. He hurried around the end of the bar and marched straight to Earl. Grasping him by the shoulders with hands the size of dinner plates, Dimitri spun him around so they were face to face. "Knock it off!" he growled. "Any more trouble and you're out for good and our deal is off. Got it?"

Earl stared back at him with vacant eyes. "He shouldn't have touched me."

Dimitri leaned into him. "And you shouldn't be messing with my customers."

Earl looked back over his shoulder. Cowboy's partner was helping him stagger out of the place, a supportive arm keeping him steady as they approached the front door.

"Satisfied?" Dimitri said angrily.

Earl shrugged impassively and brushed past him on his way back to the bar.

After resetting tables and chairs and cleaning up the mess Earl had made, Dimitri apologized to the four poker players and turned back to the bar. "Nico!" he called. "Get some music playing and bring these gentlemen fresh rounds of beer. They eat and drink for free tonight."

Nico plugged in the jukebox and Kenny Rogers picked up where he left off...*know when to walk away and know when to run*...

With the show over, everyone went back to their drinking and revelry as Nico grabbed four cold bottles and started toward the poker players. Along the way, Dimitri stopped him. "Cover for me, Nico," he said. "I've got some business to discuss with Earl."

Dimitri walked past the customers seated at the bar and motioned for Earl to follow with a wave of his hand. Earl took his glass of Diet Coke from the counter and drained it, then he rounded the bar and followed Dimitri as he turned down a short hallway and pushed open a heavy steel door that led into his office.

Earl closed the door behind him, instantly silencing the howling clamor from inside the bar. The wood-paneled room was the size of a two-car garage with framed paintings of game fish, upland game birds, and trophy whitetail deer decorating the walls. A large oak bookcase filled with hardcover books about hunting and fishing took up one entire wall. And in every corner of the room but one, stood a curved wooden display shelf crammed with dozens of wildlife sculptures made of stone, wood, and bronze. The fourth corner was reserved for a large and stunning bronze statue of a muscular dog on an attractive marble pedestal. Earl was completely taken by it. A pit bull. Its powerful figure sculpted in magnificent detail. The dog's face was set in a menacing snarl as it stood chained to a post, warning trespassers to beware.

Dimitri eased himself into a padded leather chair behind a handsome mahogany desk scattered with assorted notes and paper documents. Earl sat in the only other seat in the room, a straight-backed wooden chair situated directly in front of Dimitri. On the wall directly above Dimitri was the mounted head of a magnificent twelve-point buck.

Earl looked up at the deer. "Nico did a nice job," he said.

Dimitri smiled at the compliment. "I told you he would. My cousin, Nico, he's a natural. He's going to use it as a sample of his work when he applies for his taxidermy license."

Earl snorted a dry chuckle. "That's rich. An illegal deer as a specimen sample."

"The wardens won't know," insisted Dimitri. "He'll say he killed it during rifle season."

"If he gets caught, he better keep me out of it."

Dimitri leaned across the desk, eyes boring into Earl. "Nico is no rat. Besides, he won't get caught. You got nothing to worry about."

"That's what Billy and I thought when Wasserman and his deputy—who was also our boss at the mill—caught us with two illegal deer a couple years ago. We were fined a thousand dollars and almost lost our jobs."

Dimitri leaned back in his chair and folded his heavy arms across a massive chest. "It hasn't stopped you, though."

"I'm a lot more careful now," said Earl. "Just like with that twelve-pointer up on the wall. Wasserman would love to nail me for it, not to mention the others I got for you this year. But I don't plan on getting caught this time."

"I believe you," said Dimitri. "That's why you're working for me. By the way, is Billy Roberts still at the mill?"

Earl shrugged. "I haven't seen him in over a year. He quit the mill a few weeks after we got busted for poaching. Felt like he was being watched all the time. Couldn't take it. Why are you asking about Billy, anyway?"

"You might need some help with this next order," said Dimitri. "I found another buyer. He's from New York. Says he wants fifty deer for starters."

Earl sat ramrod straight in his chair. "You serious?"

"Of course. Interested?"

"Yeah, I'm interested, if the money is right."

"I'll pay you one hundred for every doe you bring me and two hundred for every buck with four points or more. How's that?"

"Sounds good," said Earl. "Real good. But what changed with the antlers, especially one with only four points? You never paid me more money for a buck unless it had a huge rack."

"The buyer is Chinese," said Dimitri. He said *Chinese* as if that, in itself, should have explained everything. It didn't, at least not to Earl.

"What's that got to do with it?" he asked.

Dimitri gave him a fatherly smile. "China has been using deer antlers as a medicine for over two thousand years," he explained. "They grind the antlers into a powder and sell it as a cure for all kinds of diseases like arthritis, cancer, intestinal inflammation, bacterial infections…even stress. You name it. The powder is supposed to strengthen bones and muscles too. A lot of Chinese athletes take it while they're training for a competition."

Earl scoffed at the notion. "Sounds bogus," he said. "But if that's what the man wants, it's fine with me. If it's brown it's down, especially if it has horns."

Dimitri smacked a hand on his desk in a gesture of finality. "Good! Then it's settled."

Earl nodded, then said, "So, same as always. I bring you the deer, minus the entrails, and you handle the rest."

"Yes, same as always."

Earl shot out his arm and checked his watch. "I'll be in touch," he said, standing from his chair.

Dimitri slid his chair back and stood with him. "Before you go, I want to show you something you might be interested in."

Earl looked puzzled. "You mean we're not done yet?"

"Not quite."

"What then?"

Dimitri nodded at the bronze pit bull in the corner. "I saw how you admired it when you came in."

"Yeah, it's awesome. Must be new. I never saw it before."

"New for me, yes. I bought it a month ago. But the sculpture itself is over a hundred years old."

Earl stepped over to the statue and examined it closely. The heavy bronze was partially covered with a light brown patina, which Earl thought only added to its beauty. The dog's fierce eyes exuded menace, its rigid body ready to pounce on anyone who dared to approach. Earl was captivated by its savagery.

"Do you want to see the real thing?" asked Dimitri from behind.

Earl tore his eyes from the lifelike statue and turned toward Dimitri. "More real than this?"

"Yes, the real thing, much more than a work of art no matter how exquisite it may be."

"You have a dog like this?" asked Earl in astonishment.

"Yes, and I'm offering you a part of it if you would like."

Earl was completely confused by Dimitri's cryptic rambling.

"A part of what?"

Dimitri nodded at the statue. "A part of that," he said. "Come with me. It's about to start."

Charles Valton Sculpture

Earl followed Dimitri out of the bar through a side door in the kitchen and stepped outdoors into a moonlit grassy area hemmed by a large tract of hardwoods. It was a cold night and both men were in their shirtsleeves. Earl could see his breath in the air as they walked parallel to the building until they came to a bulkhead at ground level with steel double doors. Dimitri stooped and rapped on the surface with his fist three times, pausing for a moment to rap twice more. An apparent code. After a moment, Earl heard the scrape of a bolt from inside and the door squeaked open just enough for a watchman to peer out.

"It's me," Dimitri said as he grabbed the door handle and pulled it open. A stream of light gushed forth from below as the watchman disappeared into the basement. Earl could hear a commotion of men talking excitedly as he closed the steel door behind him and followed Dimitri down a wooden staircase into a large and well-lit underground room.

The walls and floor were solid concrete. The ceiling consisted of open joists filled with layers of heavy fiberglass insulation to soundproof the area from patrons in the bar above. Centered in the room, and surrounded by two dozen men, was a "pit" built of wood, fourteen feet square with boarded sides two and a half feet high and a tight wooden floor.

The men in the room were a rough lot, it seemed, even to Earl who sized them up in seconds, seeing only one who might give him trouble in a fight. Burly hunters, loggers, and construction workers they were, all dressed in heavy wool shirts, soiled denim trousers, and rugged leather work boots. Four of the men held medium-sized dogs in their arms with pronounced cheek muscles and mouths that stretched from ear to ear. The men paid little attention to Earl and Dimitri. Instead, they were focused on a disheveled, jowly, one-eyed man standing in the center of the pit. His clothes were rumpled and streaked with black stains. He had a thatch of gray hair that looked greasy and unwashed, and his bewhiskered face bore a week's worth of white stubble. When he saw Dimitri, he reached over the side of the pit and retrieved a rusty wire cage filled with a writhing mass of brown rats. He set the cage by his feet, and the dogs, being familiar with the use of the pit, started to whine and struggle in their owner's arms.

Earl turned to Dimitri. "What's this all about?"

Dimitri raised a palm to Rat-Man, signaling him to hold up. "It's a ratting competition with four dogs," he said. "The white and brown pit bull is one of mine. Her name is Belle. The man holding her is Bowie, my handler. When I signal Rat-Man, he's going to take the rats out of the cage. There are twenty of them. One dog will be put into the pit to kill the rats while Rat-Man times him. After that, another dog goes into the pit with twenty more rats. The man with the dog that kills all twenty rats in the shortest time takes home a thousand dollars. The other dogmen will forfeit $250 each, which is what the four of us put into the kitty for the winner's prize."

"Where does he get all the rats?" asked Earl.

"Rat-Man breeds them by the hundreds in his home. They're guaranteed disease free."

At this point the dogs began to moan and fidget with excitement while the spectators grumbled for action. Dimitri took the hint and raised a hand in the air. "Rat-Man," he called. "Let the games begin."

Rat-man opened a hinged door at the top of the cage and began pulling the rats out by their tails and flipping them into the arena. While they were being counted out, those already released scurried about the floor with several climbing up on Rat-Man's legs, making him shake the beady-eyed vermin off while others sat on their hind legs cleaning their faces with their paws, oblivious to their impending doom.

The first dog brought forward was a thirty-five-pound brindle pit bull named Soldier. Upon seeing the rats, he grew excited and strained in his owner's arms while the other dogs whined in anticipation.

"Drop him in," cried Rat-Man, and Soldier was released into the pit. The rats scurried around the arena in a blind panic, while some tried to hide between small openings in the boards that hemmed the enclosure. Panting for blood with a death-stare in its eyes, the muscular pit bull chased after the rats, snatching and killing each one with a bite behind the neck followed by a furious shaking of its head. In just over three minutes, the carnage was complete with all twenty of the ill-fated rats lying dead on the floor.

Rat-Man announced the time to the audience and everyone cheered at the speed in which the rats were killed, then he picked up the celebrated dog and handed him back to his owner where several onlookers without dogs congratulated him for the dog's skill. One portly middle-aged spectator offered to buy Soldier on the spot but was promptly turned down.

Rat-Man used the side of his foot to shoot the limp carcasses across the floor like discarded pucks in an ice hockey rink until all twenty had been amassed into one corner. After placing the carcasses into a large burlap bag and setting it outside the pit, the ratting contest was repeated in the same manner three more times, with each dog's time being announced at the conclusion of the killing.

In the end, Soldier was declared the winner of the night, killing twenty rats in three minutes and nine seconds. Dimitri's Belle came in a close second with a time of three minutes and fifteen seconds. The other two pit bulls took closer to four minutes to complete the killing.

The men who had placed side bets on dogs and lost handed cash bills—mostly fifties and hundreds—to the winners while Rat-Man took a brown envelope from his back pocket and handed it to Soldier's owner. Inside the envelope was a one-thousand-dollar cash prize.

Earl said to Dimitri, "So that's what you brought me down here for, to watch a bunch of rats being killed by pit bulls? Interesting, but why should I care?"

Dimitri smiled. "That was only a preview of things to come. Now Belle will get a chance to redeem herself."

"What, more rats?"

Dimitri put his arm around Earl's shoulders and squeezed. "Watch and see."

After collecting four burlap bags filled with eighty dead rats, Rat-Man deposited them by the staircase that led to the bulkhead doors above. Then he walked into the center of the pit, pulled a stopwatch from the front pocket of his jeans, and let it dangle from its chain as he gazed at the brutal spectators waging bets and talking excitedly among themselves.

Belle was set to fight Soldier, and both dogs were known among the crowd and considered game combatants that would fight to the death if left unattended. But tonight, the rules would call for three-minute rounds with thirty-second breaks. This isn't always the case in dogfighting. Dogs are often pitted against each other until one is too injured or exhausted to continue or killed in the pit. Fights of this nature can continue nonstop for several hours unless the handlers agree to a draw in order to save their dogs from an incapacitating injury. Although the spectators would have loved to see Soldier and Belle fight like that, Dimitri considered it inhumane not to give the dogs frequent breaks.

Fighting dogs are treated like champion athletes that receive regular training. The wins in the pit often bring in thousands of dollars, so the dogs are routinely conditioned for several months ahead of a fight. A common method is to have one day of training followed by one day of rest. Belt-driven treadmills are often used, either homemade or manufactured. Most are free spinning, but some professional-grade mills are motorized and can be set to a moderate speed to keep a dog running for extended periods in order to build endurance.

Another common conditioning method is to use a spring pole to help develop jaw strength and bite force. A rope is tied to a tree branch or wooden beam in a garage or barn with a heavy spring secured to the end of the rope and another section of rope or hose added to the opposite end of the spring as an attractant that hangs several feet off the ground. Pit bulls love to pull and swing on the pole. (Both of these training and conditioning methods are used for the health and wellbeing of common household pets as well.)

Tonight, the dogs would fight until one was too injured to continue or turns. In the dogfighting world, a "turn" is when a dog turns it head and shoulders away from its challenger in the heat of the battle. Either man can call a turn on either dog, but it's up to the referee to confirm the call. If a turn is called by the referee, the dogs are separated by their handlers and brought back behind one of two "scratch" lines painted across opposite corners on the floor of the pit. The dogs face their respective corners while a thirty-second count begins. During that time, the men may cool their dogs with a sponge taken from a pail of water provided by the referee, which is visible to the spectators at all times.

When the thirty-second time is called, the men face their dogs, and the dog that turned away must cross the scratch line toward its opponent for the match to continue. If the dog fails to scratch, the fight is over with the other dog winning the prize. Although tonight's fight was set for three-minute rounds, there was no limit to their number; thus, the fighting would continue until one of the dogs was rendered unable or unwilling to continue. If a dog cannot complete his scratch, refuses to pursue a challenger, or tries to leave the pit, the match would be called by Rat-Man.

As the spectators placed their final bets, a dark-complected burly man with deep-set darting eyes knelt just outside a corner of the pit and washed the brindle pit bull named Soldier with a mixture of milk and a mild detergent provided by Rat-Man. Bowie, a broad-shouldered, square-jawed man with light blue eyes and shoulder-length blonde hair, knelt just outside a corner diagonal to the other man and washed Belle with a sponge taken from a pail containing the same liquid mixture. Each man washed down his dog under the direct supervision of Rat-Man in an effort to remove any toxic or caustic substance that might have been applied to the dog's coat (a method of cheating). Both dogs had been weighed prior to the ratting contest. Soldier, his face scarred from many battles, came in at thirty-five pounds even, Belle at thirty-four and a half. The specified weight had been set between thirty-four and thirty-five pounds; had Soldier been over the agreed-upon weight, his owner would have had to forfeit the entry fee to Bowie. Afterwards, if both men agreed, the fight could be rescheduled to a later date.

When the men were finished and had toweled off their dogs, Rat-Man took a sliver dollar from his pocket and flipped it in the air. Bowie called heads and won the toss, which allowed him to enter the pit first. Bowie stepped behind his scratch line, knelt down with Belle, and faced her into the corner while waiting for his competitor to enter.

Bell in fighting form

The dark man stepped into the opposite corner with Soldier and knelt behind the scratch line. He too faced his dog into the corner so the combatants could not see each other. A lot of money was at stake and both men were familiar with the rules: The dog and handler must remain behind the scratch line at all times until Rat-Man directed them to release their dogs. If they stepped over the line before their dog was released it would result in a loss by fouling out. Once the dogs were released, they could encourage their dogs to fight by talking, whistling or clapping, but they could not at any time touch their dogs unless Rat-Man instructed them to.

"Face your dogs!" cried Rat-Man.

Both dogs were turned to make eye contact. Muscles tensed as they struggled to be set free. There was no collar, no restraint of any kind save the grip of their respective handlers. Soldier's eyes were locked on Belle, a low growl emanating from the back of his throat. There was no barking. The dogs were silent fighters, typical of their breed.

Rat-Man looked over at Bowie and pointed at him as he held Belle securely with his muscular arms. "Are you ready?" he cried.

Bowie nodded as Belle strained to be set loose.

Rat-Man turned to the dark man. "Are you ready?" he cried once more.

The dark man nodded as Soldier struggled in his grip.

"Let go!" commanded Rat-Man.

Both dogs charged full bore across their scratch lines. You could hear them collide: a loud smacking sound as they locked up. They fought silently, so there was no fear of detection from outside. Soldier was fast as lightning and latched on to Belle's throat before she could get a grip on him. Bowie dropped to his hands and knees next to Belle and spoke to her in low tones, encouraging her to stay with the fight while Soldier's owner crouched near his dog and urged him on with shouts of approval. "Get her!" he cried. "Good boy! Get her!"

Soldier held on to Belle's throat for the full three-minute round, punishing her severely. She was on her back with

Soldier tearing at her neck when Rat-Man called time. But the brindle dog wouldn't release his grip—common in fights between pit bulls—which caused the dark man to quickly pull a breaking stick from his back pocket (a ten-inch-long rigid piece of wood with a flat point at the end) and used it to pry Soldier's jaws open. Once the dogs were separated, the men took them back to their corners and sponged them down to cool them off.

For the fight to continue, Belle would have to prove she was still game by crossing her scratch line to engage Soldier. If she failed to scratch after the thirty-second count, the fight would be over and Soldier declared the winner.

Bowie faced Belle toward Soldier and waited for the referee's call. Soldier's muscles tensed as he faced Belle. With his confidence reinforced after the first round, he squirmed in the dark man's grip, thirsting for blood.

"Fight!" cried Rat-Man.

Belle was released first followed by Soldier. Belle struck the other dog like a hammer and latched on to a front leg, flipping him hard. Soldier went for Belle's neck but couldn't get a solid grip as Belle kept him on his back, ripping and tearing at his leg with vicelike jaws.

Bowie and the dark man were on their hands and knees alongside the dogs, egging them on with shouts of praise as the spectators roared their approval.

At three minutes into the fight, Rat-Man called another timeout and both dogs were taken to their corners. Soldier was panting heavily, his injured leg held in the air. The dark man examined it closely, then looked toward the center of the pit where Rat-Man stood watching and called him over.

Both men stood face-to-face and spoke while the dark man held Soldier in his arms. Bowie knelt in his corner with Belle and watched him mouth something about a broken leg. He wasn't surprised considering the punishment Belle had given it. Then, when thirty seconds had elapsed and the dark man remained in his corner, everyone knew the fight was over.

Rat-Man turned and walked to the center of the pit. All was quiet now, for the crowd respected the rules and waited for the referee's announcement.

"We have a winner!" boomed Rat-Man. "Two game fighters gave it their all, but alas, there can only be one champion. And now, due to a fractured leg inflicted by the jaws of his opponent, and at the request of Soldier's owner, the fight is called and the winner is the white and brown dog, Belle."

A chorus of cheers erupted from the spectators, but there were many who had bet on Soldier and lost. Those men stuffed their hands in their pockets and walked away from the pit; others stood by silently as the winners collected their side-bets. Most would range between one and two hundred dollars, small in comparison to what Belle's win would fetch.

It was no surprise to Dimitri that most of the spectators had lost their money betting on Soldier. Thinking the male dog would be a superior fighter solely because he was a male and his opponent female was a fault he'd seen time and again. In the grisly world of dogfighting, a match is never determined by reproductive anatomy and biological makeup, both dogs were pit bulls of the same size and weight, and in the long history of dogfighting, there were a number of champion—and even grand champion—fighters that were females.

Rat-Man walked over to Bowie and handed him a brown envelope stuffed with two thousand dollars in cash. Although Belle was Dimitri's dog, and the money was his, Dimitri did not want the spectators to know for fear they'd suspect the fight had been rigged.

As Rat-Man went about collecting his wire cages and stacking them by the burlap bags filled with dead rats, the dark man departed with Soldier followed by Bowie with Belle along with the crowd of spectators. They climbed the wooden steps one-by-one and stepped outside into the cold night air. Earl could hear engines firing up in the distant parking lot as some of the men started for home while others returned to the bar above to continue their drinking.

Dimitri said to Earl, "Let's give Rat-Man a hand getting his cages and rats into his truck, then we'll go back to my office and finish our talk. I think you'll be interested to hear what I have to say."

There's good money to be made…" said Dimitri as he sat at his desk in his office. Earl sat in the straight-backed chair directly in front of him. "…and I'd like to make you an offer, but first I want to explain how everything works."

Earl nodded, prompting him on.

"The spectators paid me a fifty-dollar entry fee tonight," he began. "They made side bets among themselves for the dogs they thought would win. Between the ratting competition and the fight held afterwards, some men took home hundreds of dollars, but if you have a dog like Belle, you can make much more." Dimitri leaned back in his chair, folded his arms across his chest, and smiled contentedly. "I paid Rat-Man six hundred in advance for tonight. That's half of what I took in from the spectators. Bowie got the other half for handling Belle. That money plus the money from the ratting competition left me with three thousand in cash for tonight."

Earl was impressed. "It takes me more than a month at the mill to make that much money," he said.

"Some of my fights bring in as much as five or ten thousand," boasted Dimitri. "And if you have a champion pit bull—especially one that has a dozen wins or more—you can make fifty or even a hundred thousand for one fight."

Earl's eyes grew wide with interest.

"None of my dogs are of that caliber, though," admitted Dimitri. "I have ten, and I rotate them for ratting and fighting competitions. They're all pure-bred Staffordshire bull terriers—the best fighters in my opinion. The breed dates back over two hundred years to Staffordshire County, England. Bred for one reason, these dogs: to fight in the pit. It's an interesting history if you don't mind me telling you about it."

Earl nodded for him to continue.

Dimitri said, "Back in the sixteen and seventeen hundreds, it was illegal to sell meat from a bull unless it had been set upon by bulldogs. The people believed that the flesh of the bull was indigestible and unwholesome if the animal hadn't been baited by dogs. Butchers faced heavy fines and even jailtime if they killed a bull without baiting him to tenderize the meat." Dimitri jerked a thumb toward the bronze dog statue to his right. "That's what the old English bulldog looked like, nothing like the ones we see today. They were heavier, and stood far taller back then. A fearsome breed indeed.

"The baiting would be announced and townsfolk would come from far and wide to watch. It would often be held in the center of town, where a dozen or more bulldogs were brought by their owners to be set upon the tethered bull. Some of the dogs would be seriously injured or killed as the bull lowered its head and flipped them thirty or forty feet into the air. Others would be gored to death. Still, most of these fearless brutes would continue to attack the beast even when severely injured. As the bull grew weak, the dogs would grab hold of its legs and belly, tearing away at the massive animal until it could fight no more.

"The bulldogs were set against each other as well," explained Dimitri, "as dog fighting was a popular sport. Eventually, they were crossbred with English terriers in order to produce a smaller, faster, and more agile fighter. They called them bull and terriers."

Pausing for a moment, Dimitri reached down and pulled open a desk drawer and took a bottle of Johnny Walker Blue along with two glasses and set them on the desktop.

Earl's face turned sour. "You know I don't drink."

"Yes, of course. The other glass is for Bowie. He should be here soon." Dimitri twirled the cap off the bottle and filled each glass halfway. After taking a long drink, he set the glass down and refilled it. "England outlawed bull baiting and all dog fighting in 1835," he continued. "The Cruelty to Animals Act, it was called, and it made bull baiting, dogfighting, and cockfighting illegal. They were serious about it too, with large fines and even jailtime. In order to hide from the police, the

114

men had fighting pits concealed in the basements of homes and taverns, just like what I've done here."

"So, are you telling me that dogfighting is illegal here in Pennsylvania?" asked Earl.

"Not only Pennsylvania," Dimitri said, "but every other state as well. It's a violation of both federal and state laws."

"Judging by the crowd you brought in tonight, it must still be pretty popular," noted Earl.

"Yes," agreed Dimitri. "In fact, I read an article in a magazine recently that said dogfighting still has a strong following with tens of thousands of people taking part and millions of dollars laid out in bets each year."

Earl nodded appreciatively.

Dimitri said, "So, you understand, there must be a bond of trust between everyone involved here, spectators and dogmen—all of us are at risk for heavy fines and jail sentences if we get caught."

Both men looked up when they heard the bulkhead doors open above. "It's me," called Bowie. His voice was deep and assertive. "I'm coming down."

"Good!" answered Dimitri. "I have a glass of your favorite Scotch Whisky waiting for you."

Bowie descended the stairwell cradling Belle in his arms. Her neck was wrapped in a white, self-adhering fabric bandage. A small bloom of blood had worked its way through the material.

When Bowie reached the bottom step, he released Belle and she immediately bounded toward Earl at full bore. Earl stood up so fast his chair tipped backwards and crashed to the floor. He stared wide-eyed at the charging pit bull, his heart pounding in his chest. But when Belle reached him, she jumped up with her front paws planted on his thighs and wagged her tail excitedly.

Bowie and Dimitri broke into hilarious laughter at Earl's reaction "She wants you to pet her," Dimitri chuckled. "She won't hurt you."

Earl didn't appreciate the joke, and fought the urge to walk over and ram a hard fist into Bowie's jaw. He quickly shook the thought out of his head, relieved that Belle just wanted some attention. He reached down and patted her broad head for a moment. When he stopped, Belle dropped to the floor and quickly rolled over on her back with all four legs splayed to expose her soft, white underside.

"She wants a belly rub," said Dimitri. "Go ahead and comfort the poor dear."

Earl knelt beside her and stroked her belly with his fingers. Belle wagged her tail briskly, loving every second of the attention she was getting. He couldn't help but admire the dog. She was white as snow with patches of reddish-brown throughout her coat. Her right eye was encircled with a dark ring, reminding him of Pete the Dog on the *Little Rascals* movie he'd seen recently. Belle gave the impression of great strength for her size. Muscular indeed, but agile and intensely alive. With his background in wrestling, Earl was impressed by her heavy neck and powerful shoulders.

Earl stood from his crouched position next to Belle and she flipped back to her feet in an instant. Craving more attention, she began to circle him, occasionally brushing against his legs with her soft coat as he stood in front of Dimitri's desk, refusing to pick up the chair he'd knocked over.

Dimitri rose from his desk and handed Bowie a glass of Scotch. They clinked and Dimitri congratulated Bowie on his win.

"And to you as well," said Bowie.

Both men drained their drinks and Dimitri immediately took Bowie's glass and poured him another. "How bad is Belle's neck wound?" he asked as Bowie downed the amber liquid in one quick swallow.

"I've got it under control for now," he said. "Washed it out and applied an antibiotic salve, but she needs stitches. Guessing ten will do it. I'll take care of it tonight at my place. She'll be good to go in two weeks."

"Excellent," said Dimitri as he refilled their empty glasses once more. Both men sipped at their drinks this time, apparently sufficiently buzzed for the moment.

"How can a dog that fights like Belle be so friendly?" asked Earl.

"Good question," said Dimitri. "And one of the reasons why I prefer Staffords over the other bully breeds. They love to fight other dogs, but they love to love humans at the same time." He chuckled heartily. "In fact, I think this breed believes they *are* human! You saw how both men took hold of their dogs and pulled them back in the middle of a fight. Never once were they nipped by their dogs. A battle with another dog is nothing more than a good time to a Stafford."

Earl reached down and patted Belle's head. "Okay, so enough with the history lesson about pit bulls. You said you wanted to talk to me. What does dogfighting have to do with killing deer?"

"Everything and more," replied Dimitri. "Belle is for sale. I want five thousand dollars for her. But I'm willing to let you have her in trade for the fifty deer that my buyer wants."

Earl snorted bitterly. "You want me to take a dog home with me rather than get paid cash for the deer when I stand to make between five and ten thousand? Are you crazy?"

Dimitri and Bowie exchanged telling glances. "You can do much better than that with Belle," Dimitri said with an easy confidence. "Granted, it would take more time to make your money than if I paid you cash for the deer, but the sport of dogfighting is far more profitable."

"He's right," interjected Bowie. "You should listen to what he has to say."

Dimitri continued: "I have more dogs than I have time for right now. I had Belle fight tonight because I knew you would be here. I wanted you to see her in action. She's good isn't she?"

Earl nodded.

Dimitri said, "At two grand per fight, with one fight each month, you would have twenty-four thousand dollars in your pocket within one year. We've had fights here that have gone for ten thousand dollars, too. Think about it. Ten grand for one fight. And that's just the first year. With a good dog like Belle, you would still have several years of sporting ahead of you."

"And if she loses a fight?" asked Earl warily.

"There's always that risk," said Dimitri. "But if you play your cards right, and listen to Bowie and me, your wins will overtake your losses."

Earl glanced down at Belle. She was lying at his feet, looking up at him as if to say, *when are we going home?*

"Okay. I'm interested," said Earl. "But I don't know much about dogfighting or even how to get started."

"Bowie will handle that. As soon as Belle is healed, he'll bring her to your house and go over all the details with you: conditioning, feeding, fighting techniques, betting against other dogs…everything you need to know. And there would be no charge for his services."

"Sounds fair," said Earl.

"There would be some rules, of course," added Dimitri.

"Like what?"

"For the first year, all fights will be set up by me, along with your approval, of course, and you must agree to a minimum of six fights. The fights would be held here at my establishment or another place of my choosing in order to protect all of us along with my established customers. And last but not least, I get twenty-five percent of your winnings."

Earl looked at Belle and paused in thought for a long moment before turning back to Dimitri. "Okay. I'm in," he said.

Dimitri smiled enthusiastically. "Excellent!" he said. "Welcome to the world of sporting dogs!"

Billy Roberts couldn't believe his eyes when Earl Walton pulled a black Dodge Ram pickup into the service bay at the used car dealership where he worked. Billy managed to score a job there as the service advisor after he'd left the mill two years ago. Fortunately for Billy, the boss never bothered to check with the Honda dealer up the street for a job reference because they needed somebody right away and there was no time to waste.

118

George Hanks had been their service advisor for the past twenty-seven years when he suddenly clutched at this chest and dropped dead from a massive heart attack while doing a walk-around with a new customer. It was awful. When his head hit the concrete floor it cracked open like a melon. Blood was everywhere. Worse yet, the flustered car owner—a lady who happened to be one of their best customers—got so upset she fainted and fell on top of poor old George.

Billy happened to walk in and apply for a job the very next day. He was hired on the spot. It was his lucky day, he'd thought. But he couldn't help but recall what the game warden had said after he arrested him for poaching two years before: *There are two kinds of luck*, he had told Billy, *good and bad*. Billy had killed two deer with one shot that day—a lucky shot he'd thought at the time. But since it was archery season, and deer could only be legally killed with bows and arrows, Billy's lucky shot turned out to be bad luck after all, because instead of being fined for one deer, he had to pay double for two.

Yes, there were two kinds of luck, and the way Billy figured it, George Hanks' bad luck had turned right around and brought him some good luck. Some very good luck indeed. Because if the boss man hadn't been so hard up for a new service advisor, and had checked with the Honda dealer first, he would've found out about the racket Billy had going on with two conniving auto mechanics who were complicit in his scheme to charge customers for parts they didn't need. If a heater fan stopped working but only needed a squirt of oil, Billy would sell them a new fan. If a hose was leaking coolant, it would be time for a new radiator. Brake pads with fifty percent wear would always be replaced with new pads, even though they were good for thousands of miles. Most customers were never the wiser, and the more work Billy could convince his customers that their vehicles needed, the more money he could put into his pockets.

Billy was six-foot-two with the ropey build of a farm boy. He had a generous mop of sandy-brown hair that fell in different directions over his head as if he had just rolled out of bed. His heavy-lidded green eyes were dark and mysterious, adding to his sleepy-looking countenance.

Billy had a sixth sense about which customers he could take advantage of. When he spotted one, all he needed to do was what he did best: lay on his mesmerizing, folksy charm, and they went along with everything he said. His dreamy-eyed smile captivated most of the women—even the grandmas. And most men fell for his robust handshake and pleasant, *I'm-looking-out-for-you* sales pitch. But all good things must come to an end. And it did for Billy Roberts when the manager's sister was charged two thousand dollars for a transmission job she didn't need. Billy had no idea who she was. Because her last name (in marriage) wasn't the same as the manager's, he never connected the two. When the manager got wind of the fraudulent transaction, he was fired immediately.

Billy had the same racket going on here as he had at the Honda shop before, but this time there was only one mechanic involved along with him. It was a smaller shop, so he wasn't making the same money from the scams as he had been at the Honda dealer, and he was at a point in his life where he needed all the money he could get hold of.

Earl Walton and Billy Roberts were the same age and had graduated from the same high school where both had been outstanding athletes: Billy a star basketball player and Earl a state champion wrestler. A few years after graduation, both men happened to run into each other at the mill when Billy started working there after being fired from the Honda dealer. After a short conversation over lunch at the cafeteria one day, Billy invited Earl to go hunting with him; hence, Earl had been with him when he'd killed two deer with his Winchester XTR Featherweight 30-06 out of season.

Casey Grant, their boss at the mill, was bowhunting nearby and suspected foul play when he heard the blast from a high-powered rifle. Casey didn't like the idea of poaching, so he jumped in his car and went looking for whoever might be hunting in the area. It didn't take long before Casey spotted Billy's truck: a jacked-up blue and tan Ford F-150 with chrome rails—the same one that he'd seen parked at the plant on numerous occasions. Casey called the game warden the following day, which started an investigation rolling.

Earl blamed Billy for ratting on him after Wasserman came to his house and arrested him for assisting in the unlawful kill of two whitetail deer (and he was right). Fortunately, Billy was able to lie his way out of it by convincing Earl that it was their boss, Casey Grant, who had turned him in.

Billy was deathly afraid of Earl Walton. Although they were on good terms, Billy never forgot the night that they ran into a grassy field to retrieve the two deer he had shot. Billy stood back and watched Earl gut the first deer with a pocketknife and ram his bare arm into the chest cavity all the way to his elbow, then with one quick pull, he ripped the entrails out of the carcass as easy as shucking an ear of corn. "Don't be afraid of a little blood," he'd scolded Billy. Earl's eyes bulged in their sockets under a brilliant full moon, and he looked like a madman. Billy felt like he could see directly into his soul at that moment, and what he saw chilled him to the bone.

Earl Walton shouldered open the door and swung out of his Dodge Ram. He strolled toward Billy Roberts as if he owned the place, ignoring the other two service reps assisting customers with their cars as he passed them by. The dealership smelled of raw gasoline, motor oil, and exhaust fumes. Earl couldn't figure out why Billy wanted to work in a place that smelled so awful. It had to be bad for his health. Billy was standing at the opposite end of the dealership with an attractive female customer in her mid-thirties whose car needed a tune-up along with an oil change and filter. She knew the oil change was due because the *service oil* indicator in the instrument panel had been shining bright red for two weeks. The tune-up would be an extra hundred dollars, and Billy had just finished assuring her that she needed one—even though the engine only had a few thousand miles on it—when he saw Earl pull into the shop.

Earl stood off to the side as Billy was writing up a work order for his overcharged customer. He glanced up at Earl several times as he jotted down the details, annoyed that he'd invaded his workspace without an appointment or notice of any kind. They hadn't seen each other since Billy had quit his job at the mill, and he was both puzzled and annoyed by Earl's unannounced visit.

Billy finished writing and smiled at his customer. "All set," he said. "There's a comfortable waiting room through the door on your right where you can get coffee, snacks, and watch TV while you're here. It should only take an hour or so to get you back on the road."

He watched as she walked into the waiting room, then turned to Earl. "If you need your truck serviced, it's best to call for an appointment first," he said coldly.

"But I want to talk to you about something," urged Earl. "It'll only take a minute."

"I'm working," said Billy, clearly irritated. "Come back around five when I'm off."

Earl pushed on: "I walked into a sweet deal last week, Billy. There's some good money to be made. Something you might be interested in. Can you break away so we can talk about it?"

Billy looked around the service area. There were only two other cars inside, and both customers had service reps helping them.

"We're not too busy right now," he said. "But I only have a few minutes. Let's walk over to your truck; make it look like you're a customer so the boss doesn't get on my case. The guy's a real micromanager. Can't stand him."

Earl went to his truck, popped the hood, and stood on the driver's side of the engine bay while Billy stood across from him on the passenger's side. "Okay, what's going on?" asked Billy.

Earl said, "I've been shooting deer for a guy I know. He sells the meat and pays me cash for every one I bring him. Been with him for the past two years. He usually doesn't pressure me, just takes what I can get him. Twenty or thirty a year for his regular customers and he's happy." Earl looked around the service area, then leaned toward Billy and lowered his voice. "He met some Chinese guy who wants fifty deer, and that's just for starters. He especially wants deer with horns. I got ten so far, but it's going slow because I'm working alone. I could use a spotter."

"Whoa!" protested Billy. "Why me?"

"I don't know anyone else I can trust. Besides, I don't expect you to do it for nothing. I need forty more deer. I'll pay you fifty dollars for every one we kill. That's two thousand dollars in your pocket for a few night's work."

Billy thought about the offer for a moment, then said: "What about Wasserman and his deputy, Casey Grant? How do we make sure they won't catch us again?"

"Got that taken care of, my friend. Grant fell off his ladder pulling leaves out of his gutters a few weeks ago and broke his leg. He's still in a cast and can't drive. His wife takes him to work every day." Earl snorted a bitter chuckle. "When I see him hobbling around on crutches at the mill I have to look away so he doesn't catch the smile on my face. I'd like to kick his crutches out from under him just to watch him fall on his butt."

Billy grunted in agreement.

"I have a scanner in my truck that has all the police and Game Commission frequencies on it," continued Earl. "If they get a call about shots fired, I'll hear it. I also found a place where I can keep out of sight and watch Wasserman's house with binoculars. I only shoot on nights when his patrol car is there. He parks it in the driveway. Makes life so much easier for me."

"It sounds like you got it pretty well figured out," said Billy. "And I can sure use the money. I'm not exactly making a fortune here."

"So, you're in?" asked Earl.

"Yeah. I'm in. When do we start?"

I had just wheeled into the state game lands in the northern end of my district and was backing toward the deer pit with a highway killed deer when a call came over my radio about a hunting accident. The dispatcher gave me the location, which was a good twenty miles away, and I radioed back advising him that I would soon be on my way to the scene.

As I dragged the deer carcass off my big game rack and dumped it into a pit that had been dug into the earth with a backhoe, I couldn't help but recall how I disposed of highway kills when stationed near Philadelphia. In those days (1970s) my deer were taken to a rendering plant. The building was huge, as the plant employed over a thousand people. The back entrance was where local farmers entered if they had a dead cow or other deceased livestock to dispose of, and I used it as well. A concrete shaft roughly fifteen feet long by twelve feet deep protruded from the rear wall of the building that I would drop my deer carcasses into. A mechanical door would then descend to the bottom of the shaft and push the carcass inside the building for processing. I'll never forget the time I pulled into the plant only to see a mound of dead dogs and cats the size of a large round hay bale piled-up next to the shaft. My guess was that the doomed pets had come from an overburdened animal shelter. Most were guiltless victims of families who'd grown tired of them I supposed, their miserable faces frozen into a macabre collection of grimaces and howls of utter panic.

I knew that rendering plants collected raw matter from the livestock and poultry industry as well as waste from supermarkets and restaurants to convert it into paints, varnishes, and other items. For decades afterward, I couldn't help but think about that gruesome sight whenever I had to paint a room or put a fresh coat of varnish on wood trim that had weathered.

With the deer disposed of, I climbed back into my patrol car and traveled south to the center of my district. The hunting accident had occurred on a twenty-acre property along a rural and seldom used road flanked by open woodland on both sides. As often happens, the police had been called first and by the time I arrived an ambulance had already taken the victim to a nearby hospital. There was a state police car parked along the road with a trooper standing by. A young man, he stood ramrod straight with his flat-brimmed Stetson fitted perfectly upon his head. He waved me over and I pulled behind his vehicle and parked.

"Good afternoon warden," he said as I approached. "Been waiting for you."

"Appreciate that," I said. "Do you know what happened here?"

He nodded. "Spoke with the victim right before the ambulance arrived. He was headed home on his ATV when he saw a nice buck and took a shot at it with his revolver. He said he missed the deer and when he holstered his gun it went off and put a bullet into his lower leg."

"How bad is it?" I asked.

"Not good," said the trooper. "Thirty-eight caliber slug hits you in the calf, point blank…ouch! He's suffering, that's for sure."

I nodded in agreement.

"I'm no hunter," he said, "but I'll say one thing: your job has gotta be more dangerous than mine with all these yahoos running around in the woods shooting at everything that moves. I must have heard a dozen shots while I was waiting for you. Don't these guys have to take classes before they get a hunting license? I mean, how dumb can you be to shoot yourself in the leg like that? He had to have his finger on the trigger when he holstered his gun."

I said, "We have mandatory hunter education classes for all first-time hunters, but some hunters get so excited when they see a nice buck they forget themselves and accidents happen. And you're right about the potential danger," I added. "I've always thought my chances of being accidentally shot by an overanxious hunter were a lot higher than being shot on purpose by somebody who doesn't like me."

The trooper pursed his lips and shook his head. "No way I'd want your job. Too many crazies out there."

I shrugged off his comment. "Most hunters are good sportsmen," I said. "But there's always a few…"

"I have the victim's gun and holster in my trunk," he said as he turned and popped open the lid. The trooper pulled out a Taurus .38 Special revolver with a six-inch barrel along with a leather western style holster and handed them to me. The holster had an exit hole in the toe from where the bullet had gone through. I thanked him for securing the evidence, then turned and started toward my patrol car.

"You stay safe out there, warden," he said.

"Thanks," I called over my shoulder. "You do the same."

The hospital receptionist was a rotund woman in her late forties who sat at a brown mahogany desk stacked with papers as she examined the screen on her computer. She looked up as I approached, her eyes focusing on my state-issued green Stetson and then to the badge on my uniform jacket. "Game warden?" she said with mild curiosity. "Can I help you?"

"I'd like to talk to the gunshot victim that was brought in earlier."

"The state police have already done that," she said dismissively. "The patient is resting now."

"I understand, but I still need to talk to him," I said. "He was deer hunting and it falls under my jurisdiction."

Her mouth curled into a pout. "The poor little deer," she said shaking her head with pity. "How can anyone shoot them? They're so beautiful."

I stared at her in silence. After realizing I wasn't going to respond, she turned back to her computer screen and scrolled down a long list of names. "Second floor, room two-thirty-two," she said without looking at me. "Elevator is down the hall and to your right."

"Thank you," I said.

"Hmpf!" she muttered icily. "Now that he knows what it's like to be shot with a gun, maybe he'll leave the poor deer alone."

Ryan Stead looked up at me and groaned as I walked into his room. He was in his mid-twenties and covered up to his neck with a gray hospital blanket. There was a half-full IV bag hanging above his head from a pole-stand. A transparent plastic tube ran from the bag to the back of his wrist where a clear solution dripped into a vein. A heart monitor stood on a shelf behind him emitting a subtle steady beep as the green rhythm strip that ran across its screen spiked at regular two-second intervals.

"State game warden," I said.

"Yep. I know who you are all right."

"How are you feeling?"

"Okay. They got me pretty doped up right now. Going in for surgery soon."

"I spoke with the state police," I said. "Just wanted to make sure everything they told me was correct."

He shrugged. "I'll tell you what I told them: I took a shot at a buck and missed. The gun went off when I stuck it back in my holster."

"Did you have your finger on the trigger?"

A half shrug told me he wasn't sure.

"Was the hammer cocked?"

"Don't know."

"It's illegal to have a loaded firearm in a vehicle, including an ATV," I said.

"I didn't know that."

"It's also illegal to use a vehicle to hunt."

Stead arched his eyebrows in surprise. "Whoa! I wasn't looking for a deer," he said. "I was on my way home to get something to eat when I saw a nice eight-pointer. I mean, who wouldn't take a shot at a deer like that?"

I really didn't have a solid case against him for using a vehicle to hunt. There was no witness to dispute his words, so any attempt at a prosecution would have been baseless. I needed more in order to feel right about a five hundred dollar fine. Besides, if he was telling the truth, and there was no intent to hunt from a vehicle, most hunters would have done the same thing.

"How long have you been hunting?" I asked.

"About ten years," he said.

"A hunting digest is included with your license every year. Have you ever read it?"

He shook his head. "Not really. I mean, I do check the seasons and bag limits, but that's about it."

I wasn't surprised by his answer. Over the years, I'd found that many seasoned hunters are convinced they're familiar with game laws only to learn that a rule or statute has changed over time.

"There's a lot of information about rules and regulations inside as well," I said. "Looks like you'll be laid up for a while; it might be a good time to look it over."

Stead nodded that he would.

"I'd like to take a look at your hunting license," I told him.

"It's on my jacket," he said, chinning toward the wall behind me. "Look for yourself. It's hanging inside the closet."

I stepped over to a narrow cabinet with a single door built into the back wall of his room. Inside was a pair of denim jeans with a bullet hole in the calf area, a heavy plaid shirt, socks, leather work boots, underwear, and a brown Carhart jacket with a hunting license pinned to the back. I pulled the license out of its holder and opened it and saw that his deer tag was still attached and unused. Taking a notepad and pen from my jacket pocket, I wrote down the information required for an accident report as well as any citations I might file, then I stuffed it back into the holder and closed the closet door.

"No orange vest or hat?" I said.

Stead closed his eyes and expelled a weary sigh. "Guess not."

He looked like he was getting tired, and I could understand why considering the trauma he'd been through.

"Thanks for your cooperation," I said. "I'm going to go now so you can get some rest."

"You gonna write me a ticket?" he asked.

"Yes, but only for having a loaded gun in your ATV. It'll be a written warning for no orange clothing."

"Thank you," he said.

"And you're on thin ice with the deer," I cautioned. "There are laws about when you can shoot at game when you're on an ATV. Better read up on them."

"Yes, sir, and thanks again…really. I always thought game wardens were hard-nosed Gestapo types." He realized what he just said and swallowed hard. "I mean, that's just what I heard, not that I ever thought that."

"We actually have hearts, believe it or not," I said with a chuckle. Then: "Oh, and you can have your gun and holster back when this is all settled; just be sure to have the trigger mechanism checked by somebody who knows what they're doing."

"I sure will," Stead replied. "I sure will."

On my way out of the hospital, I spoke with a floor nurse about Stead's condition. She told me that after the bullet had entered his calf it lodged in his ankle. He was scheduled for surgery later in the day so they could extract the slug and would need several months of therapy before he could walk without some means of artificial support. I thanked her for the information and continued down a long hallway until I came to the receptionist at the front desk again.

"Did your friend learn his lesson?" she asked as I passed by.

I turned and faced her. She held a half-eaten sandwich in her hands; a fast-food bag on her desk indicated that it was pulled pork.

"My friend?" I asked.

She gave me a smug grin. "Game wardens encourage men like him to go out and kill innocent birds and animals, don't they? I think that's disgusting."

I turned to leave, paused, then wheeled around to face her. "How's that sandwich?" I asked.

129

She squinted at me warily. "Why?"

"I toured a meat packing plant once," I said. "They specialized in pork products. Every day hundreds of innocent pigs were unloaded from a tractor-trailer and lined up nose to tail as they entered the plant through a narrow chute. Once inside, they were shot in the head with a stun gun and hung upside-down on a conveyor belt where a man in hip boots and a rubber apron stood on a floor covered with gore and slit their throats one by one. Blood gushed from their necks like Yellowstone geysers. It was quite a sight."

She stared at me in stunned silence and set her sandwich on the desk.

"Enjoy your lunch," I said.

With the hunting accident behind me, I resumed my patrol for the day and drove toward a remote section of my district where I'd been getting a number of calls about night shooting. The area in question consisted primarily of farmland interspersed with small tracts of forest. There were lots of deer to be found, as hunting pressure was low here since most of the farms were posted against trespassing. It wasn't that the farmers didn't like hunters; they simply wanted them to ask permission first so they would know who was on their property and when they would be there. Unfortunately, many hunters mistook their signs to mean that they did not allow hunting at all. As a result, the deer population had increased tremendously over the years, and crop damage was heavy at times. Still, the farmers frowned upon poachers shooting deer at night for fear a stray bullet might enter a home or barn. Others worried that a hunter might mistake their livestock for a deer, or worse, target their animals intentionally.

While cruising along a narrow gravel road hemmed by open grassy fields, I spotted a dead deer lying in a meadow on my right. A good hundred yards from the road, its white belly was plainly visible even at that distance. I pulled over and parked at the edge of the field, knowing that the ground was frozen enough to support the weight of my patrol car, and walked out to inspect the carcass.

The deer, a small doe, had been shot thought the chest. A visible trail of blood confirmed that it had been shot on the opposite side of the road, some distance away, and had run off only to die where I found it. It had to have been done at night, otherwise, the poacher would have seen it run across the road and drop in plain sight. Evidently they were in a hurry, and once the deer ran off, decided to move on and look for another target. I examined the carcass for a telltale slug but the bullet had gone clean through, so I dragged it a short distance into a wooded ravine at the edge of the field and left it for the vultures and other critters to feed on.

On the way back to my patrol car, I decided to return to the area after nightfall. The deer was a fresh kill; less than twenty-four hours had passed since it had been shot. If the poachers returned, I wanted to make sure I was close enough to catch them in the act.

Not long after continuing my patrol, a call came over my radio advising me to contact the State Police Crime Lab regarding the evidence I'd submitted weeks earlier. The incident had played on my mind ever since discovering the decapitated deer in my driveway. I was certain Butch Stryker was behind it, and hoped for confirmation by the lab. If so, it might be enough to put him behind bars for a while.

I made a three-point turn and wheeled toward the state highway where a convenience store I knew about had a phone booth outside.

The parking lot was full when I pulled in, but nobody was using the phone booth, so I parked next to it, dropped a quarter into the slot, and dialed the number for the State Police Crime Lab. The phone rang twice when a male voice answered: "Trooper Samuels speaking."

I identified myself and asked about the icepick and greeting card I had submitted for fingerprints.

"That was quick," remarked the trooper. "I just called the Game Commission a little while ago."

"It's personal," I said, explaining why.

"Yeah, I guess it *is* personal," he remarked after hearing what had happened. "Would be for me too. We lifted a nice thumb print off the greeting card. Nothing on the icepick. Whoever did it doesn't have a criminal record, I can tell you that. Print drew a blank. No match came up in our system."

I thanked Trooper Samuels for the information and hung up. I was both surprised and disappointed. Not only was my prime suspect innocent (at least for this crime, anyway), it left me at a total loss for who might be responsible. All game wardens have a few enemies; it comes with the territory, but we generally know who they are or at least have a strong suspicion. In this case, I had no idea.

Thinking of you. I couldn't get those haunting words out of my head, and the agonizing thought of what might be planned for me on his next visit played on my mind.

Earl and Billy had just finished tossing their third doe into the back of Earl's pickup when they saw headlights ahead, and they were coming fast. Billy stood at the tailgate in momentary shock. Neither of them expected company in such a remote area, especially at one o'clock in the morning.

"Don't just stand there; get in the truck," shouted Earl.

Billy ran to the passenger door and yanked it open and tumbled inside. Earl walked rather than ran like Billy, then he climbed into the truck and sat there as calm as a toad basking in the sun.

"Let's go Earl!" cried Billy. "It might be the game warden!"

"Notice anything about the headlights?" asked Earl as he keyed the engine.

"We ain't got time for guessing games," whined Billy. "We gotta go!"

Earl waited until the lights were on top of them before dropping his pickup into gear with an audible clunk. Seconds later, a Mazda Miata shot past them like a bullet and disappeared into the night leaving a wake of choking brown dust.

Earl shook his head and smiled sadly. "Hope you didn't pee yourself, Billy."

Billy glared back at him. "That's not funny, Earl. How did you know it wasn't the game warden, anyway?"

"The headlights," he said. "Wasserman drives a Ford Bronco. Those lights were too low to the ground, so I knew they came from some kind of sports car. Besides, lawmen come up from behind you for a stop, not from the front. It's too dangerous. If it was the warden, he would have waited until we drove past him and then red-lighted us."

"Maybe," grunted Billy.

"I'm surprised you didn't know about the headlights considering you work at a car dealership," Earl said sarcastically.

"Maybe not, but I did recognize the clunk I heard when you put your truck into gear. Better stop by the shop and have your transmission checked. The last thing we need is for your truck to break down while it's loaded with dead deer."

Earl and Billy continued their deer killing spree with Billy sitting in the passenger seat with his arm out the window shining fields while Earl drove down one lonely road after another. There were plenty of deer to be seen, and they had killed two more, but Earl wanted to see some horns, so he passed up all the antlerless deer standing in fields until Billy spotted a nice six-pointer.

Earl pulled to the road's edge and stopped while Billy kept his light on the deer. It paid them no mind as it grazed in a grassy pasture fifty yards to their right. Earl shifted into park and killed the engine. Then he eased his door open and quietly slid out with a scoped Ruger M77 30-06 and steadied himself across the hood of his truck for a kill shot. Perhaps sensing its fate, the buck raised its heavy head and gazed at Earl as he rested his finger on the trigger.

KaPow!

As with the five deer before, Earl's shot was true, and his deadly missile tore through the buck's heart, dropping it instantly.

Billy switched off his spotlight, jumped out of the truck, and raced for the deer with Earl seconds behind him. Earl dropped to his knees, unzipped the deer with a razor-sharp Buck folding knife and yanked out its entrails, after which both men grabbed the deer by its legs, front and rear, and hustled it back to the truck.

It took all of five minutes before they were on their way.

As always after shooting a deer, Earl drove several miles away before searching for another kill, and before long the men had taken two more buck deer: a four pointer and another six pointer for a total of three bucks and five does before calling off their hunt. They'd pushed their luck far enough and didn't want to stay out any longer.

"I gotta see somebody," said Earl as he turned onto the main highway and started toward town.

"Now?" whined Billy. "It's two-thirty in the morning!"

"He's expecting us. It's Dimitri, our buyer. His bar closes at two, so the place will be empty and we need to get rid of these deer."

"Dimitri! I know him," said Billy. "Been to his place a few times before. I'm surprised he's into this kind of stuff."

"He's into a lot more than bartending, I can tell you that."

"Like what?"

Earl glanced over at Billy, then back to the road. "I'll tell you about it after we drop off these deer."

"Then we get our money, right?"

"Not exactly," said Earl.

The unlit macadam parking lot was empty except for Dimitri's Ford F350 when Earl and Billy pulled in. It was parked conveniently in the center of the darkened lot with the tailgate down. Earl backed his Dodge Ram up to the Ford's bed and parked. All four men climbed out of their trucks and faced each other under a brilliant half-moon. The night was cold and still.

"Who's that with you?" grunted Dimitri.

"It's Billy Roberts," said Earl.

"Ah! I've seen you in my place before," Dimitri said to Billy. "Now I can put a name to the face."

He turned to Earl. "How many?"

"Five doe and three buck."

"Nice haul," replied Dimitri. "It pays to have some help. I know you and Billy have worked together in the past. Now I see why. At this rate you should have all fifty killed in a couple more weeks."

Earl nodded. "They're like fleas on a dog's back."

Dimitri said, "Speaking of dogs, Belle is set for another fight. And with Apache, no less."

"That's right."

"You're taking a big risk," cautioned Dimitri. "Apache is a bigger dog."

"You approved it didn't you?"

"I did. It's set for next Saturday night. But there's still time to call it off, or at least postpone the fight for a later date when Belle has more time in the pit."

"Don't worry about Belle," grunted Earl. "We'll be there. Just make sure the other guy is too."

Dimitri blew a heavy sigh. "I think you're making a mistake," he cautioned. "Apache has had many fights, and he's a killer."

"You have a dog now?" asked Billy as they drove toward Earl's single-wide trailer on Cemetery Road.

135

Earl nodded. "Yep, she's a champion fighting dog. I got her from Dimitri."

Earl told Billy about the illegal ratting competitions and dogfighting racket that Dimitri had going on at his bar and made him swear he wouldn't tell anyone. Billy had never seen him so excited before. In fact, he'd never seen Earl excited about much of anything before.

"You gotta see it for yourself," Earl assured Billy. "I mean, the way these pit bulls tear into each other. They'll fight to the death if you let them. It's unbelievable. And the rats, too. They grab them in their jaws and with one shake, bam! Just like that, the rat's dead." He gave Billy a wolfish grin, then looked back at the road ahead. "They remind me of me," he said. "When you find a rat you kill it."

Billy got the message loud and clear: Earl wasn't talking about killing four legged rats. It was meant for him, and his chest tightened with fear.

W hen Earl's Dodge Ram pulled into his driveway and parked, Billy was surprised to see a medium-sized dog scurry out of a thirty-gallon plastic barrel lying on its side on his front yard. The dog was tethered to a heavy fifteen-foot tow chain.

"That's Belle, my fighting dog," said Earl as he set his brake. "Hop out and say hello to her."

As Billy and Earl approached, Belle ran to the end of her chain wagging her tail with excitement. Earl bent down and removed her collar while Belle licked his face with her long tongue. Once free, she ran around both men in wide loops, circling them several times before charging at Billy only to jump up and plant her front feet on his thighs with her tail wagging in delight.

"She likes you," said Earl. "But then, she likes everybody."

"And this is your fighting dog?" asked Billy. He was clearly bewildered.

"Yep. She's my ticket to fame and fortune, and that's what I wanted to talk to you about."

Billy bent over and massaged Belle's muscular cheeks with his fingers. He could feel old fighting wounds that had scabbed over on her face and neck as she purred with delight at his touch. "I'm listening," he said.

"I can't pay you because Dimitri didn't pay me," Earl said. "And the reason is because I made a deal with him to take Belle in trade instead of money for the deer."

Billy pushed Belle off his legs and backed away from her. "But I need that money," he groaned. "My mom is sick and can't work. We have bills to pay and things are getting tight at home."

Earl shot a menacing glare at Billy. "I got it covered!" he snapped. "You'll get your money right after the fight next week. I got five thousand dollars—my entire savings—riding on it, and I don't need you hounding me right now."

Earl's fists were clenched. His face twisted into an ugly scowl.

"Okay, Earl. Okay," pleaded Billy. "I trust you, man. I can wait."

"**W**e need snow," complained Earl as he and Billy cruised down a dark country road on the following Friday night. It was two o'clock in the morning. "If we had snow on the ground, the deer would stand out like flies on a wedding cake, and we wouldn't need a spotlight to tell the world we're out here."

Billy was shining an adjacent field with a gloved hand to protect him from the biting cold. But there were no deer to be seen, so he flicked off the light and set it on the floor between his boots and rolled up the Dodge Ram's window from the icy weather.

"We have three bucks in the back; that makes fifteen deer for the week," said Billy. "How about calling it a night. We still have to get them over to Dimitri's and I worked a long shift at the shop today. I'm beat."

Earl continued driving without a word in response.

"Besides," Billy continued, "it's freezing cold out there and Belle has her fight tomorrow. Maybe you should head back early and get her inside. Warm her up. Loosen her limbs a little."

Earl looked over at Billy and grunted. "Know why I keep her outside? Because it makes her strong. It's the same reason I run her on a treadmill every day and keep her tied to a tow chain. It helps build muscle and stamina. You don't know nothing about fighting dogs, Billy. But then, most people don't, so I can't blame you."

"Guess not," said Billy.

Eighteen hours later, Earl Walton drove his Dodge pickup over to Dimitri's bar with Belle curled on the seat between them. It was a twenty-minute drive, and Billy gently kneaded the top of Belle's head with his fingers as he gazed out the windshield at the starry night. He'd look down at her occasionally, and Belle, feeling his gaze, would stare up at him with unblinking eyes. Billy thought she looked sad, and wondered if she sensed the looming fight.

"I think Belle knows," he said to Earl. Belle's ears perked up at the sound of her name.

"Knows what?"

"About the fight. She looks sad."

"Dogs don't look sad or happy, Billy. It's all in your head."

Billy disagreed but kept it to himself. Earl seemed edgy about the fight and he didn't want to set him off. Instead, he changed the subject: "I've never seen a dogfight before. This will be my first."

Earl grunted in response and tightened his grip on the steering wheel. Billy kept his mouth shut for the rest of the drive.

The parking lot was lit up by a half dozen pole lights when Earl pulled into Dimitri's bar. The place was so packed with cars and pickup trucks that it was difficult to find an opening. Earl circled the lot until he found a spot between two pickup trucks at the back end. He eased his Dodge Ram between them and parked. When he switched off the engine, Belle stood on the seat, sneezed hard twice and shook herself off, her ears flapping against the sides of her head like sheets in a windstorm.

Earl picked her up and held her under his right arm while he exited the truck. Billy followed him as he strode toward the bar, wondering what would happen to Belle when she faced Apache.

Billy stood back and watched as Earl rapped on the steel double doors that led to the basement of the bar. Three slow knocks with his fist followed by two more, a simple code, Billy knew, to ensure those inside that it was safe to open.

After a moment, one of the doors popped just enough for the watchman to see outside. A bright shaft of light filled the narrow opening, and Billy could hear the murmur of male voices from below.

"You can come in," the watchman said to Earl. "Who's that with you?"

"Billy Roberts," answered Earl. "Dimitri should have given you his name."

"He did," acknowledged the watchman. "Come in, both of you."

Earl lifted the heavy steel door and followed the guard down the stairwell with Belle tucked under his arm. Billy followed Earl and closed the door behind him.

A hush came over the room as Earl entered with Belle. All heads turned in anticipation of the fight. They wanted a look at the dog that was to confront Apache. Some had seen her before but many had not. The news of the fight had brought a large crowd, some from as far as Philadelphia, New York, and New Jersey.

Billy did a quick head count. Fifty men had gathered around the fighting pit. They were a rough lot. Most were dressed in heavy plaid shirts and khaki work pants with hunting boots, but some sported neatly pressed dress pants and wore stylish button-down solid-color shirts from Haggar, Kenneth Cole, and the like. Billy was amazed. He could feel the excitement in the air. This would be a night to remember, he thought. But things were about to go south quickly, and little did he know just how right he was at the time.

There would be no ratting contest tonight. It was all about the fight between Apache and Belle. Many thousands of dollars would be won and lost, and the men were anxious for the show to begin.

Apache stood in the back of the room behind an eager crowd of spectators with his handler. He was a smooth-coated dog, like Belle, but weighed forty pounds compared to her thirty-four. His coat was the color of rust with a well-muscled body that showed great strength for its size. He had a broad skull with very noticeable cheek muscles, a short foreface, steadfast eyes, and cropped ears that projected a devilish and most menacing appearance. His short, muscular neck widened toward powerful shoulders. Unlike Belle, his tail was docked short. His front legs were straight and set wide to provide for a broad and powerful chest. Black fighting scars punctuated his face and body.

Rat-Man stood in the center of the pit and held up both hands to quell the crowd as Belle and Apache were washed down by their handlers. Eager for the fight to begin, the men grew quiet and turned their attention to the referee.

"Gentlemen!" he boomed. "I'm proud to announce tonight's fight! In the corner to my left, we will have the pit bull called Belle. A female scrapper with three wins to her name. She's a local dog, and she weighed in at thirty-four pounds, even."

With that, the crowd cheered enthusiastically, which made Billy smile and feel more confident about the approaching fight. Earl, untouched by the applause, glared at the spectators as if they were no more than a gang of unwelcomed intruders.

"And in the corner to my right," announced Rat-Man, "we will have the pit bull called Apache. Brought here all the way from Philadelphia, Apache weighed in at forty pounds and two ounces. A male scrapper with seven fights and five wins to his name."

The crowd offered a mixed applause. Although Apache was favored to win by most of the men, many had placed bets on Belle and thus kept silent for the out-of-town challenger.

Rat-Man waited for the applause to die, then instructed the handlers to enter the pit. As was custom, Apache's handler entered first with his dog as he was a guest who had traveled from afar. He was short and squat with a heavy beard and a mop of brown hair that looked like it had been cut from under a bowl placed over his head. Bowie entered the pit next with Belle in his arms. He wore clean indigo-blue denim jeans and a buckskin shirt made of suede leather fringed at the chest and shoulders.

Rat-Man looked at Bowie. "Are you ready?" he cried.

Bowie nodded, and Belle, sensing the fight was at hand, struggled in his brawny arms.

Rat-Man turned to Apache's handler. "Are you ready?"

The man nodded once as Apache struggled to be set free from his grasp.

"Face your dogs!" cried Rat-Man.

Both dogs were set down. Apache crouched low, his eyes thirsting for blood. Belle strained in Bowie's grip, wanting nothing more than to latch on to her opponent and take him down. Both had transformed into canine gladiators. There was no barking, no growling or whining. They would battle in silence, typical of dogs bred to be fighting machines.

"Let go!" shouted Rat-Man.

Both dogs charged toward each other and locked up. Apache, a throat fighter, and taller than Belle, latched on to the back of her neck before she could get hold of him. Belle struggled in his grip, but Apache's powerful jaws would not let go. Bowie dropped to his hands and knees alongside Belle and encouraged her to fight while Apache's handler crouched near his dog and urged him on. "Kill her!" he cried. "Good dog! Sic her, boy!"

Apache worked on Belle's neck and chest for the full three-minute round, battering her severely. Belle had always fought dogs equal to her size and weight, dogs that she could handle. Apache proved to be a different matter, and Earl began to have doubts when the first three-minute time was called.

After a thirty-second rest, both dogs were let go, and Belle, having no fear, charged full bore across the pit. She ducked under Apache, rolled him over with her head, and latched on to a front leg. Apache went for Belle's chest, as she was on top of him, which made for an easy mark. The fight was vicious and bloody, like two men going at it with knives in their hands. At the end of the second round, both dogs were battered when taken to their corners to be washed down by their handlers.

Billy never expected the fight to be so brutal and sadistic. He had seen dogs fight before but never like this. In his experience, dog fights were between two hounds that had tangled in a back yard somewhere and lasted only a few seconds with one running off holding its tail between its legs. This was different. And it sickened him.

The fight went on for five more rounds. Both dogs battled savagely for the entire three minutes until pulled off and brought to their corners. When Rat-Man called time, they'd dash across their scratch lines and hit each other like two freight trains colliding.

The spectators loved it. They crowded around the pit, the ones closest to it leaned over the boarded sides to cheer for their favored dog. Earl stood back, impassive as always, and watched Apache and Belle go at it. The only thing on his mind was the money he'd make if Belle won. She was a source of income and nothing more.

Billy stood next to Earl with his stomach wrenched into a sickening knot. Bile built up in his throat until he thought he might puke. He was witnessing the most vile and disgusting spectacle he'd ever seen in his life.

At the end of the seventh brutal round, both dogs were brought to their corners. Apache, torn and bleeding, teetered on his feet as he stood and faced Belle in the opposite corner.

Belle was on her belly behind her scratch line, broken and exhausted, her white coat stained with blood. After thirty seconds, Rat-Man called time, and Apache stumbled lamely across his scratch line toward Belle. Belle tried to stand but fell back on her belly and began to crawl toward Apache.

Bowie, realizing she was too injured to continue, grabbed hold of Belle and pulled her back behind her scratch line. Then he stood and waved off the referee, signaling that the fight was over. There was a howling roar from the spectators, some in favor while others jeered and booed at Bowie's move.

Earl was enraged. Bowie had no right. Belle was *his* dog, and she'd crossed her scratch line in an attempt to fight again when he stopped her. Realizing Bowie had just cost him five thousand dollars, Earl leaped over the pit's wooden barrier and charged at him.

Bowie, suspecting Earl would do just that, turned to defend himself, but Earl was on him in a flash and knocked him to the ground with a vicious left hook, rendering him unconscious from the blow.

Seething with anger, Earl grabbed Belle by the back of her neck and shouldered his way through the crowd with Belle dangling in his grip like a limp dishrag.

Billy stood among the rowdy spectators, dumbfounded as he watched what was happening.

Someone from behind shouted, "He's gonna kill 'er." Another cried, "Dead dog, for sure!" And many in the crowd roared with approval.

Billy, having no doubt they were right, rushed through the clamoring mob toward Earl.

Somehow, he had to stop him!

Earl was out the steel bulkhead doors by the time Billy reached the staircase. He screamed for Earl to stop as he scrambled up the steps, hoping to reach him before he harmed Belle.

Earl stood twenty feet away with Belle lying motionless at his feet as Billy charged out the bulkhead doors into the cold and cloudless night. "What did you do to her?" he screamed.

"Nothing yet," grunted Earl. "What's it to you, anyway?"

Billy started toward him, knowing that Earl could break him in half but willing to take the risk if he had a chance to save Belle. "Don't you touch her," he hissed.

Earl snorted a vicious laugh, his cold eyes boring into Billy. He reached into the edge of his boot and produced a razor-sharp double-edged dagger. "Want some of this?" he said. "Then come and get her."

Billy froze. "You're going to kill her, aren't you?"

Earl looked down at Belle; she was motionless. "It'll be quick," he said. Then he knelt by her side with the dagger clenched in his fist.

"Get away from the dog, now!" came a voice from the open bulkhead doors.

Billy spun around as Earl slowly rose to his feet and glared at the intruder.

Billy remembered him from the crowd below. Unlike the others, he wore a black motorcycle jacket. His steely-eyed gaze focused on Earl, a heavy twelve-inch KA-BAR knife was clenched in his right hand, the same knife that had been issued to the Marines in World War II.

Earl's eyes flicked from the knife to the biker's unwavering stare, calculating whether he was serious or bluffing, when a sudden screech of tires came from the parking lot behind them.

A mass of police vehicles, both state and local, began to block the exits, their red and blue emergency lights blazing against a blackened sky. Doors swung open as dozens of armed men stormed from their vehicles and rushed toward the bar.

They would be on them in seconds; there was no time to lose. Earl turned and ran into the adjacent woods hoping to escape.

The biker sheathed his knife and strode toward Billy. "Get the dog and come with me."

Billy stood frozen with fear.

"Now!" he commanded as he moved past Billy and ducked into the woods.

Billy picked up Belle and cradled her in his arms as he followed the biker along a foot path through the trees. In the distance, he could hear the lawmen announce their presence as they swarmed through the open bulkhead doors: "State police! Put your hands in the air!"

The biker soon came to a two-track and veered off to follow it with Billy close behind. They didn't go far when they stopped to uncover an ATV concealed under a pile of brush. The biker climbed onto the machine. "Sit behind me," he said. "There's room for you and the dog. I'll go slow."

Billy held Belle under one arm and grabbed the biker's shoulder for support with the other as he mounted the extended seat. He pulled Belle close when the engine roared to life.

The biker put his machine into gear and eased it through the woods along the rugged and broken trail. He traveled for a hundred yards or so until he came to a seldom-used gravel road and stopped.

"I have folks who live close by," he said over his shoulder. "They're about two miles from here. I'm going to speed up a little bit, so hold on to the dog when I start moving."

"I will," said Billy.

The biker switched on his headlights and pressed lightly on the thumb-throttle for a smooth start. They traveled for twenty minutes, passing a half-dozen homes along the way. Billy could see lights in their windows, and he envied them. He wished he were home too, watching TV with his mother over a bowl of buttery popcorn without a care in the world.

The following morning, I received a phone call from the state police informing me that three untagged, freshly killed buck deer were discovered hanging in a barn while they were executing a search warrant on a property suspected of possessing dogs for the purpose of dogfighting. Agents from the US Department of Agriculture (USDA) assisted in the search and took possession of the carcasses hoping I could come by and pick them up.

"I can stop by for them today," I said. "Whose property were they found on?"

"Suspect's name is Dimitri," said the trooper. "Owns a bar out in the boonies."

"I'm surprised," I said. "I had no idea there was a dogfighting ring in my district."

"Nobody at the barracks knew either. We were notified about it yesterday straight from headquarters. The USDA had an undercover agent working it for over a month, and we assisted them in a raid last night. It was a good bust. We arrested fifty-three men and confiscated sixteen thousand dollars in cash along with some handguns and one pit bull that was beat up pretty bad. The USDA agents also searched Dimitri's property and removed ten pit bulls that were tied out on heavy chains and living in barrels for doghouses. Most of the dogs were battle-scarred pretty bad. You gotta be a real creep to do something like that."

I nodded in agreement although the trooper couldn't see me.

"Where can I find Dimitri?" I asked. "I want to talk to him about the deer."

The trooper chuckled. "Well, you're in luck, 'cause he's here at the barracks along with his partner in crime—calls himself Bowie. You might want to talk to him too. He's been asking for a game warden all morning long."

The interview room at the barracks was Spartan by design, consisting of four white walls, two folding chairs, and a single wooden desk. Under the desk, a heavy chain was bolted to the floor to accommodate shackled prisoners. A one-way observation window was situated on a wall to our right. It looked like a mirror from where we sat. I motioned for Dimitri to sit at the desk, his back to the wall, as I pulled a plain wooden chair from the corner and sat across from him.

"Tell me about the deer," I said, taking a notepad and pen from my uniform shirt pocket.

Dimitri's brow wrinkled in mock surprise. "What deer?" he asked. It was the same response I'd heard from a hundred men before.

"The three buck deer that were hanging in your barn," I said (at the time, I knew nothing about the deer that Earl Walton and Billy Roberts had brought him).

He looked relieved for a moment, then nodded knowingly. "Ah, yes. *Those* deer. One is mine, one is Bowie's, and the other one my cousin, Nico killed."

"They're all untagged," I said.

Dimitri leaned back in his chair and shrugged coolly. "The excitement of the moment," he said. "We simply forgot."

I wrote the names he gave me on my notepad and looked up at him. "So, when I check state records, I'll see that all three of you have hunting licenses, right?"

"Of course!"

I didn't believe his story. "Hoping to catch him in a lie, I asked, "Which one did you kill?"

Dimitri thought for a moment, then: "I have nothing more to say right now. If you want more information, you'll have to talk to my attorney."

"You'll be hearing from me again," I said, rising from my chair. As I did, a trooper who had been watching through the two-way mirror stepped into the room and escorted Dimitri out the door and down a long corridor, only to return a short time later with Bowie.

"He's been asking for you," said the trooper as he ushered Bowie into the room."

147

I pointed to the chair opposite me and Bowie took a seat. As he did, I noticed that the left side of his face was bruised and swollen.

"You wanted to see me?" I asked.

"Yeah. I got some information you'll want to know about."

"I'm listening."

"You know a guy named Earl Walton?" he asked.

I nodded. There was instant recognition with the name. Walton had a violent and explosive temper, and it was one of the few times in my career that I thought I might have to draw my gun in order to defend myself against a suspect.

Bowie rubbed his swollen jaw for a moment. "Well, him and Billy Roberts are shooting deer at night. Killed a bunch of them, too."

"How do you know that?"

"Never mind how I know," he said, eyeing me warily.

"Then why are you telling me about it?"

"See my face?" he said angrily. "Earl Walton cold-cocked me last night. Knocked two of my back teeth out, all because I tried to save a dog from being killed in the pit." He frowned and shook his head. "Why kill a good fighting dog when it can live to fight another day? I mean, where's the profit in that?"

Dogfighting disgusted me, and I wanted to reach across the table and grab him by the throat. Instead, I shook the thought out of my head and asked him what else he knew about Earl and Billy.

"That's it," he grunted. "Now go out there and catch them. They both got away last night—probably the only ones that did when the cops showed up."

I stood from my chair. "One last question," I said to Bowie. "Were you deer hunting recently?"

He looked at me as if I'd just grown two heads. "Where did you get that idea? I don't hunt."

"There were three untagged bucks hanging in Dimitri's barn last night," I said. "He told me that he killed one and that you and Nico killed the other two."

Bowie scoffed. "I'll give you this," he said. "And only because I warned Dimitri that he was crazy to have anything

148

to do with that psycho, Earl Walton. Those three deer came from Earl and Billy. We didn't kill any of them."

I was on my way out of the barracks, eager to catch up with Earl Walton or Billy Roberts, when the sergeant in command called me into his office. "I have some information for you, warden," he said.

I stepped into his office as he walked back to his desk and grabbed a sheet of paper from a manilla folder. Turning, he asked, "Do you know a man named Earl Walton?" It was the second time I'd heard the question since I stepped into the barracks, and it caught me off guard for a moment.

"I do," I said.

He nodded. "Thought you might. My men found him hiding in the woods behind the bar last night. He was arrested for participating in a dogfighting exhibition and consequently fingerprinted." He handed me the paper he'd taken from his desk. It was a document from the State Police Crime Lab. "When we entered his prints into our system, we got a hit," he continued. "As you can see, Walton's thumbprint matched the one that was found on a greeting card that you submitted to the crime lab recently. Congratulations, warden, looks like you got your man."

I was shocked. I had foolishly narrowed my suspects down to two men, and when I learned that one of them had moved out of the state, I convinced myself that it had to be Butch Stryker. It was a mistake on my part and a lesson to be learned.

Billy's Ford pickup was parked by his house, a modest brick home surrounded by a large tract of hardwoods where he lived with his mother. I eased my Bronco down the long driveway and parked behind it. It was the same truck he had when I arrested him two years ago.

I slid out of my patrol car and walked to the front door and knocked. I was in full uniform and suspected that Billy or his mother would have seen me coming from one of several windows facing the driveway.

Within seconds, Billy came to the door and opened it wide. "I knew you would be coming for me," he said, looking over my shoulder to see if I brought reinforcements. "Just didn't think it would be this soon."

"Mind if I come in?" I asked.

Billy stepped back from the door and I walked into an open living room, surprised to see his mother lying on a linen sofa with a pit bull cuddled next to her. Its face was peppered with wounds; its chest wrapped in a white fabric bandage. The dog looked over at me and wagged its tail, refusing to move from his mother's side. Given its appearance, I had no doubt that it was a fighting dog.

"Hello, officer," his mother called. Her voice was choked and weak. "I'm sorry I can't get up; I broke my back and have to stay right here on this couch."

"I'm sorry to hear that," I said.

She smiled a thank you. "Why don't you go into the kitchen with Billy. I know he did wrong. We talked last night. He told me all about what happened, and he's going to answer all of your questions for you."

I followed Billy through the living room and into the kitchen and we sat across from each other at a round wooden table.

He said, "I figured Dimitri or Bowie would talk after the raid last night. How much did they tell you?"

"They told me everything," I said falsely. "Now it's your turn."

Billy sucked in a long breath and slowly let it out. "I only did it because my mom is hurt bad," he said. "She can't work, and we got fifteen thousand dollars in hospital bills to pay. We're behind on our house payments too. So when Earl came by the shop and offered to pay me for helping him kill some deer, I told him I would."

"How many did you and Earl kill?"

Billy stared at the ceiling while counting mentally. "Ten or eleven, best I can remember," he said. "But Earl killed a bunch more before I started riding with him. I don't know how many, but he planned on killing fifty for some Chinese guy that Dimitri knew."

The news angered me, and I could feel the hairs on the back of my neck stand up.

"Earl's been killing deer for Dimitri for years, but not me," Billy said. "I'm being totally honest with you about what I've done because I don't want you coming after me for what Earl did before we hooked up."

"Fair enough," I said. "But you've got more problems coming your way. Dogfighting is a felony. I know you were there last night, and I saw the injured pit bull when I walked in your house. You're looking at state and federal dogfighting charges, Billy. That's jail time."

"Whoa!" cried Billy. "She's not *my* dog, Belle belongs to Earl."

"Then why do you have her?"

"Because he was gonna kill her after she lost the fight with Apache. That's how I got away. Earl dragged her outside and was gonna stab her with a knife when this biker dude stopped him."

Billy told me about the incident and how he and the biker escaped on an ATV and went to the biker's parents' house with the injured dog.

"His mom and dad were real nice folks" said Billy. "His mom used to work for a veterinarian. She went into a back room and brought out a black bag filled with medicines and sutures and stuff. She stitched up a bad wound on Belle's side and put salve on the wounds on her face and neck. Belle just laid there and let her do it. Not a whimper came out of her. After Butchy's mom got Belle patched up, his dad drove me home with her."

"Butchy..?" I said.

"That's what his mom kept calling him—Butchy."

"What did he look like?"

151

"Tall," said Billy. "Over six feet for sure. On the lean side with long red hair." Billy paused for a moment, then let out a light chuckle. "His ponytail kept brushing against my face the whole ride to his parents' house. Made my nose itch."

I sat in stunned silence. *Butch Stryker... it had to be!*

"Do you know him?" asked Billy. "You look surprised."

"We've met," I said.

"You gonna arrest me?" he asked. "Because I can't go to jail. My mom needs me here with her."

"I'm not going to drag you off in handcuffs, if that's what you mean."

He looked relieved. "How much is my fine gonna be?"

"I don't know yet," I said. In truth, there was little I could do. Billy's confession, in itself, was not enough to convict him in a court of law. I needed more. And without witnesses to verify his story, I had nothing unless Earl, Dimitri, or Bowie— his partners in crime—were to testify against him. The odds of that happening were incredibly low considering they'd be incriminating themselves with their testimony.

"I think we're done here for now," I said, rising from my chair. "I appreciate your honesty and your cooperation."

Billy stood from his chair along with me. Then he stuffed both hands in his pockets and stared at the floor for a moment. "There's something I need to ask you," he said.

"Go ahead."

He swallowed hard and raised his head, and I watched the rims of his eyes begin to water up. "Will you take Belle with you...please? She can't stay here with us."

I was caught completely off guard. "What am *I* supposed to do with her?" I said. "She's a fighting dog. A pit bull."

"She's a sweet dog, really," he said. "She loves everybody she meets. You saw her with my momma. Belle won't leave her side because she knows she's hurt. Dimitri and Bowie trained her to fight other dogs, not people." He paused and wiped a tear from his left eye. "Maybe you could find her a new home. She might need more vet care, and we can't afford it. Besides, if Earl finds out she's here, there's no telling what he might do. I'm afraid he'd try to take her, or even kill her."

I knew enough about Earl Walton to know Billy had every right to be fearful. Still, it put me in a difficult position.

"I'll take her," I said. "But she's going to the humane shelter."

"But they'll kill her," he pleaded. "She's a fighting dog."

I shook my head. "No, they won't. I'll speak with them—tell them to call me if nobody adopts her. I won't let them put her down."

"Promise?"

"You have my word."

Belle was curled up sound asleep on the passenger seat of my state issued Ford Bronco as I turned off a side road toward the local animal shelter. Her breathing was heavy, punctuated by an occasional deep sigh as if her dreams were burdened by confusion. I could understand why. In less than twenty-four hours she'd gone from Earl Walton and the fighting ring to Stryker's place, and then to Billy Roberts's house. Now she was with me, and I felt a pang of guilt knowing I was about to drop her off at the pound as if she were no more than an afterthought.

I glanced over at her as I drove. A pretty dog indeed, with her snow-white coat mottled by patches of reddish-brown fur. Adorable, really. She was lying on her belly with her front feet tucked under her chest like a cat. I reached over and rubbed the top of her head with my fingers and she drummed her tail against the passenger door.

Soon the animal shelter appeared just ahead. I pulled into the parking lot and killed the engine. There was no turning back now I thought as I pushed open the driver's door and stepped out. It was a beautiful sunny day under a cloudless blue sky—a day that would make anyone glad to be alive. The animal shelter was flanked on both sides by a chain link fence crammed with dozens of wire pens accompanied by pacing dogs, mostly of mixed breeds, longing to be taken home by somebody…anybody, I supposed.

I stepped around to the passenger door and opened it. Belle looked up at me with questioning eyes, her naturally perked ears held low against her head. "It's all right," I whispered as I picked her up and held her close. But Belle sensed that it wasn't all right, for she quivered in my arms and nuzzled my chest with her nose as I carried her toward the shelter.

Halfway to the door, I suddenly remembered the day when I came upon that dreadful pile of unwanted dogs and cats at the rendering plant, their tortured faces frozen in agony.

And I turned away.

"**H**oney, I'm home," I called as I opened the front door and stepped into my house. "I have somebody I want you to meet. Her name is Belle!"

Belle, happy at last.

EPILOUGE

A court jury convicted Dimitri and Bowie of aiding and abetting in the possession and training of dogs for purposes of an animal fighting venture. They were sentenced to six months in prison and fined five thousand dollars. Both men were also convicted of possessing three unlawfully killed deer and fined fifteen hundred dollars and had their hunting privileges revoked for three years.

Apache's owner was convicted of sponsoring a dog in an animal fighting venture and fined five thousand dollars.

The other fifty-some-odd spectators caught in the raid were convicted of knowingly spectating at a dog fight and fined one thousand dollars.

Earl Walton was convicted of sponsoring a dog in an animal fighting venture and fined five thousand dollars. In addition, he was convicted of unlawfully killing a deer, wanton waste, and harassment for the decapitated buck he placed on my driveway and was fined fifteen-hundred dollars with his hunting privileges revoked for three years. No other poaching charges were brought against him due to a lack of witnesses willing to testify.

Nico confessed to me that the twelve-point buck head he had mounted and then hung on the wall in Dimitri's office was from the decapitated deer that Earl Walton left on my driveway. Nico was fined five hundred dollars with no chance of obtaining a taxidermy license in the near future.

Billy Roberts and Butch Stryker were never linked to the dog fighting exhibit the night of the raid.

I was able to confirm that Billy Roberts' mother had been unemployed for several months and that they had significant mounting debts as a result of her physical rehabilitation. Due to these circumstances, coupled with the fact that I had no witnesses who would testify against him for poaching, no charges were filed.

William Wasserman, a third-degree black belt in the Korean martial art of *Tang Soo Do* and a former national bodybuilding champion, has written thirteen books about his life as a state game warden. He received numerous awards for his work in wildlife conservation, including the United Bowhunters of Pennsylvania Game Protector of the Year Award, Pennsylvania Game Commission Northeast Region Outstanding Wildlife Conservation Officer, National Society Daughters of the American Revolution Conservation Medal, and the Pennsylvania Trappers Association Presidential Award. Wasserman has been published in several national magazines including *Black Belt, Pennsylvania Game News, Fur-Fish-Game, South Carolina Wildlife, International Game Warden,* and *The Alberta Game Warden.* Wasserman retired from the Pennsylvania Game Commission after thirty-two years of dedicated service and lives in South Carolina with his wife, Maryann.

POACHER JUSTICE

WILLIAM WASSERMAN